Johanna Davis

Machine Knitting

to suit your baby

Johanna Davis

Machine Knitting

to suit your baby

Pelham Books

PELHAM BOOKS

Published by the Penguin Group
27 Wrights Lane, London W8 5TZ. England
Viking Penguin Inc., 40 West 23rd Street, New York, New York
10010, USA
Penguin Books Australia Ltd. Ringwood, Victoria, Australia
Penguin Books Canada Ltd, 2801 John Street, Markham, Ontario,
Canada L3R 1B4
Penguin Books (NZ) Ltd, 182–190 Wairau Road, Auckland 10, New
Zealand

Penguin Books Ltd, Registered Offices:
Harmondsworth, Middlesex, England

First published 1988

Made and printed in Singapore
by Kyodo Shing Loong Printing

Typeset by Goodfellow & Egan (Phototypesetting) Ltd, Cambridge

British Library Cataloguing in Publication Data

Davis, Johanna
    Machine knitting to suit your baby.
    1. Infants—Clothing   2. Knitting, Machine
    I. Title
    746.43'2   TT637

ISBN 0-7207-1730-2

Contents

Introduction

Machine knitting to suit your baby is a book for all those who wish to machine knit something special for a baby, or indeed, a child. All baby patterns can easily be scaled up to fit the larger tot. What better way to regain your knitting confidence, if you have lost it, or even if you haven't, than by trying out an idea on a manageably small scale? What better opportunity for experimenting with a new stitch idea, or technique, than to try it out on a miniature jersey, which if it works you can adapt for yourself, and if it fails, all that has been lost is a little time and wool?

Another enormous advantage of knitting for a baby is the satisfaction of using all those small oddments of wool for some special purpose. If the balls are too small for a garment, a knitted toy, in the form of a mobile, makes an excellent present for a baby.

This is a book for every knitter. It is for anyone owning a basic, single-bed knitting machine and needing ideas, patterns, and variations on those patterns both in size and yarns. It is not difficult to knit very original and seemingly complicated designs using the simplest techniques; and even though a time-consuming technique may seem daunting if miles of knitting is needed, for something small, it seems quick and effortless.

Just as there are infinite varieties of pregnant mothers, so too are the images these mothers have of their offspring infinitely varied. When her child is very small a mother has, almost without exception, the only opportunity to dress her child exactly as she wants; a situation many mothers want to exploit. The country mother may want her baby to be warm and happy in wonderful tweedy knitted outfits, admirably suited to her lifestyle. The sophisticated urban mother possibly sees her offspring reflecting her own chic, in elegant coats or lush dark jerseys. The mother permanently clad in overalls may well see her baby also in overalls – but warm and cheerful in a bright striped cardigan. I have used only a selection of the infinite images mothers might have of their prospective offspring but they can all be adapted to suit any baby's personality.

Of course, it is most important that the knitted present is not only appropriate for the particular baby, but also for the season. A padded mohair coat, for example, would be singularly inappropriate in summer, whereas an extravagant white cotton knitted dress would not. However, there are certain garments which are essential all the year round. The cardigan is one such garment, a vital part of any baby's wardrobe if they live in an unpredictable temperate climate. Although babies need an extraordinary number of clothes because they must be changed so often, they do grow at an incredibly rapid rate, so that garments become redundant far too soon and any clothes that they can grow into are always very acceptable, particularly if they have been made as a special present.

Pregnant mothers themselves may not always feel like sitting at a machine to knit, even though the knitting required is minimal, but there are armies of prospective grandparents, friends, aunts and all those eager to honour the arrival of a new baby.

Johanna Davis

1 Five Basic Shapes

Because babies grow at an alarming rate, it is essential, before attempting to knit anything for any size of baby, to familiarize yourself with their extremely curious shape. Around their middles they are enormous, but they have narrow shoulders, short necks and large, unstable heads. And there are other important factors to be taken into account. Draughts must be avoided and openings are essential to facilitate changing the baby frequently. But the first prerequisite of making clothing for a baby is to understand the idiosyncrasies of a baby's proportions. I have suggested five basic patterns (baby blocks) so that shapes in the subsequent chapters will appear totally familiar. These basic blocks will be used throughout the book and adapted to form new shapes. Once the knitter is familiar with these blocks, he or she should have no difficulty in inventing new patterns, using any of them as a guide.

After taking trouble over knitting baby clothes, do take care of them. Without good care they inevitably change into felted doll's clothes so always wash and dry them very carefully.

1. Slash Neck Block

The first block is the simplest of all. This jersey needs only four rectangles: front, back and two arms; with buttons along both shoulders to the neck. Depending on your confidence, you could shape the sleeves and add built-in mittens resembling miniature pillow-cases. If you fear draughts around the neck, a separate tube can be knitted to make a cowl neck or hood. By dividing the front, this block is particularly suitable for use as a simple jacket pattern.

2. Crew Neck with Set-in Sleeves Block

This jersey can have a small front or back opening or an opening all the way down the front, making it a cardigan. For extra warmth and draught exclusion the neck can be increased in height or a shirt collar can be attached with a button opening down the front.

8

3. Raglan Sleeves Block

This block can be modified in much the same way as block 2. It also has the added advantage of being particularly suitable for big, knitted necklines.

4. Wrap-over Shoulder Block

This shape is perfectly suited to accommodate a baby's large head and small neck, and does not need any buttons.

Note: Any of these jersey blocks can be elongated to make a baby bag or romper suit.

5. Leggings Block

For the bottom half of the baby the most important shape is the leggings which need to be capacious enough to accommodate all the inevitable layers of nappy and other undergarments that babies have to wear. Leggings must fit snugly around the ankle in order to exclude draughts, or feet can be added to prevent the 'solitary sock' predicament.

Each basic block has been explained bearing the beginner in mind, and all the patterns can be adapted to fit any size of baby. Simply use the measurements given in a pattern for the size/age of baby you want to knit for and either increase or decrease your chosen pattern measurements accordingly.

The block diagrams given for each garment are for your guidance. If your tension varies from the tension given, then use the measurements on the block diagrams and your garment should turn out the correct size and shape. Most of the garments can be knitted on any single-bed, standard gauge knitting machine. For chunky single-bed machines use double knitting yarn or yarn doubled. There are several patterns included for double-bed machines and for machines with punchcard and intarsia facilities.

**All measurements on block diagrams
are in centimetres.**

1. SLASH NECK BLOCK

Materials
Knitted in Lister Motoravia 4 ply wool: 75 gms fisher-man. 6 small buttons. See photo, page 10.

Size
To fit baby aged up to 3 months (50cm).

Tension
First, knit a 4cm **tension swatch**. Pin it out on an ironing board without stretching, and steam press. When dry, count stitches and rows. This *must* be done for *every* garment you knit, whatever yarn you are using. Individual machines vary, and no two knitters knit exactly the same on the same machine so the knitting can also vary, even if the tension dial number used does not.

For this basic shape the tension should be:
Tension dial number 6
12 stitches = 4cm 3 stitches = 1 cm
16 rows = 4cm 4 rows = 1cm

Note: Always work out tension over 4cm for greater accuracy. To correct tension: too few stitches or rows to the cm, then you need to make stitches smaller so decrease number on tension dial. Too many stitches or rows to the cm, then you need to make stitches larger so increase number on tension dial.

Machines
Any domestic single-bed machine.

Back: First knit the rib, as follows. Change tension dial

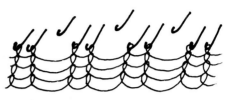

diagram 1a

cast on position of needles for rib

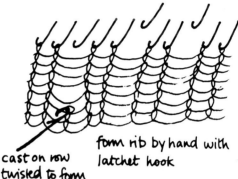

knit 10 rows on pairs of needles only

form rib by hand with latchet hook

cast on row twisted to form first row of rib

to at least one number higher than that used for the main body of the garment, i.e. dial number 7. Bring out 66 needles. Push out of action every third needle. Cast on all those needles in action (see diagram 1a).

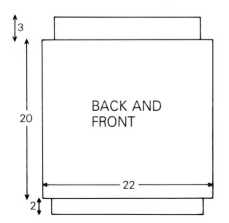

BACK AND FRONT

3

20

22

2

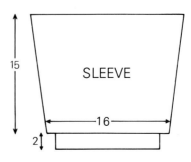

SLEEVE

15

16

2

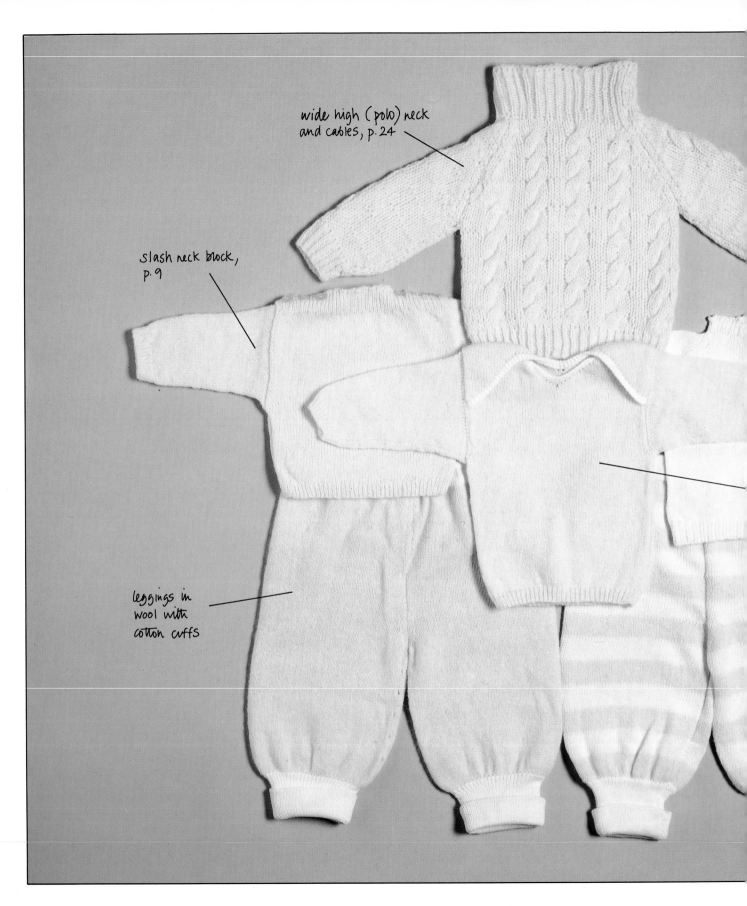

wide high (polo) neck
and cables, p. 24

slash neck block,
p. 9

leggings in
wool with
cotton cuffs

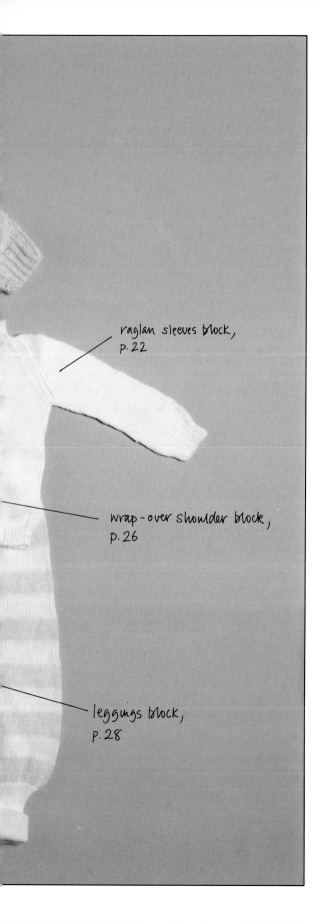

raglan sleeves block,
p. 22

wrap-over shoulder block,
p. 26

leggings block,
p. 28

diagram 1b

Knit 10 rows (2cm). With latchet hook/tool twist yarn in between the pairs of needles and form rib by hand (see diagram 1b). Place newly-made stitches on the empty needles. This method of ribbing may seem time consuming, but for a small garment it is worth the trouble as it makes a very good rib. A quicker alternative to a rib is a hem which is described in the pattern for block 2 on page 13.

To knit the main body of the garment change tension dial number to 6. Knit 80 rows (20cm).

To knit top rib, change tension to 7 or 8, remove every third stitch from its needle, and push needle out of action. Leave the needleless stitches if they appear not to be dropping, otherwise place pins through each (see diagram 2). Knit 15 rows (3cm); with the latchet hook pick up all dropped stitches to form rib, place newly-made stitches on empty needles and cast off.

diagram 2

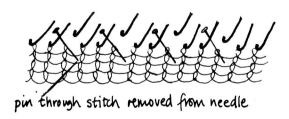

pin through stitch removed from needle

Front: Knit exactly as back until you reach the top rib. Rib as for back for 10 rows (2cm). At both sides of knitting transfer every third stitch to adjacent needle three times to form three buttonholes either side (see diagram 3). Continue rib for 5 more rows (1cm), pick up dropped stitches as for back, and cast off.

diagram 3

1   2   3

for buttonholes transfer 3
stitches onto adjacent needles

1   2   3

needles 1, 2, 3 transferred to form
button holes in rib

diagram 4

centre

sleeve –
place overlapped
front and back
onto sleeve
hanging on
machine

overlapped rib
on central needles

centre overlapping ribs

Sleeves: Bring out 48 needles (16cm) and push back every third. Knit rib as for back. Change to tension 6. Over the next 60 rows (15cm) you need to gain 12 stitches.* Knit 60 rows (15cm) increasing one stitch at both sides of knitting every 10 rows. You should now have 60 stitches.

At row 60 pick up the back and front and overlap their top ribs by 1cm. Then hook the stitches of the overlap onto the central needles of the sleeve (see diagram 4). Continue hooking evenly on both sides the stitches from the back and front onto the needles of the sleeve. Knit one row, and cast off. This makes a much neater finish than sewing by hand.

Repeat for the second sleeve.

To finish: Pin knitting flat on an ironing board and either using a steam iron or an iron over a damp cloth, press into shape. When dry, pin and sew seams together edge to edge (see diagram 5). This gives a flat seam which is better and less bulky on small garments. Attach buttons opposite buttonholes.

If the garment has been knitted in oiled wool it must be washed thoroughly in warm soapy water, rinsed, rinsed again in fabric conditioner and squeezed out carefully in a towel. Gently pull into shape and dry flat.

*Note: To calculate the number of times you need to increase:

diagram 5

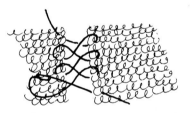

sewing up seams edge to edge

a) Find the overall number of stitches to be added. In this case 12 (60−48). Therefore you need to increase 6 stitches each side over the 60 rows.

b) Divide the number of rows by the number of increase stitches. In this case 60÷6=10. Therefore you must increase one stitch at both sides every tenth row.

The same process can be applied for calculating the number of times you need to decrease.

It's a good idea to have a calculator handy if you're not particularly numerate!

2. CREW NECK WITH SET-IN SLEEVE BLOCK

Variation 1: with shirt collar and stripes

Materials
Knitted in Lister Motoravia 4 ply wool and Brockwell Wools 4 ply and 2 ply cotton: 25gms 2 ply white cotton, 50gms of fisherman wool, 50gms of white 4 ply cotton.

Size
To fit baby aged 3–6 months (60cm).

Tension
Dial number 6
2.75 stitches = 1cm
4 rows = 1cm

Machines
Any domestic single-bed machine.

Front: Cast on 74 stitches (27cm). Knit hem as follows: using tension 3 and 2 ply cotton, knit 13 rows (2cm). Change to tension 4 and knit 1 row (for fold in hem). Change to tension 3 and knit 13 more rows. Pick up onto existing row of stitches the cast on row (see diagram 6). Change to tension 6 and return row counter to 0. Knit in stripes (10 rows 4 ply wool, then 10 rows 4 ply cotton) until row 64 (16cm). Work, including hem, should measure 18cm. Make armhole shaping by casting off 4 stitches row 64 carriage side and 4 stitches row 65 carriage side (66 stitches). At row 68, to make the front opening, bring all needles left of centre to hold position. Continue striping, knitting right side only – 26 rows until row 92 (6.5cm). Over the next 16 rows hold 18 stitches. Begin by holding 2 stitches row 92 right of centre, then 1 stitch every row until row 108. Thread a length of odd yarn through the 18 held neck stitches to prevent dropped stitches on shaped side and remove them from the machine. Cast off 15 stitches of knitted shoulder right side. Push back out of action all right side needles. Put row counter back to 68. Using needles left of centre make left side: cast on 4 extra stitches right of centre so that there are 4 extra needles in action right of centre. This is for the buttonhole placket. Knit exactly as right half (placing buttonholes 2 needles from the centre on rows 70, 80

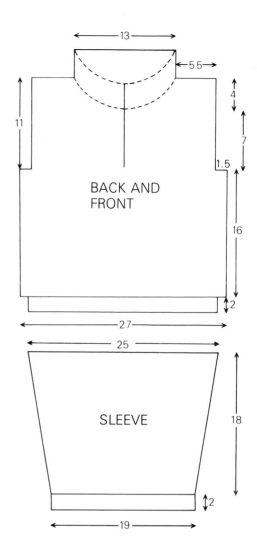

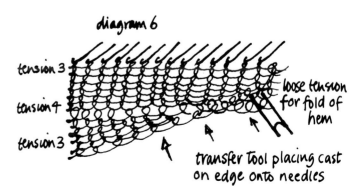

diagram 6

tension 3
tension 4
tension 3

loose tension for fold of hem

transfer tool placing cast on edge onto needles

13

and 90) until neck shaping on row 92. Change carriage to left side of machine. Over the next 16 rows hold 18 stitches plus the 4 extra stitches on the right of centre, until row 108. Hold the 4 extra stitches plus 2 left of centre on row 92 then 1 stitch every row until row 108. Cast off 15 stitches for right shoulder (leaving 18 held stitches on machine for right side of neck). Cast off the extra 4 stitches right of centre before knitting left collar.

Left side collar: Change to tension 3 and using 2 ply cotton knit 20 rows. Knit 1 row at tension 4, change to tension 3 and knit another 20 rows. Pick up stitches from first row of collar onto the last row knitted and cast off.

Right side collar: Having replaced onto the machine 18 stitches from the thread for right half of neck, repeat as for left side collar.

Back: Cast on 74 stitches (27cm). Knit hem as for front. Change to tension 6 and knit in stripes as for front, until row 64 (armhole). (Work, including hem, should measure 18cm.) To shape armholes, cast off 4 stitches row 64 carriage side and 4 stitches row 65 carriage side. Continue striping every 10 rows until row 108. Cast off 15 stitches (5.5cm) both sides for shoulder seams. This leaves 36 stitches (13cm) for back collar. Change to 2 ply cotton and tension 3 and knit 20 rows. Change to tension 4. Knit one row, change to tension 3 and knit 20 more rows. Pick up stitches from first row of collar onto needles and cast off.

Sleeves (method A): Tension 3, cast on 52 stitches (19cm) in 2 ply cotton. Knit 13 rows, change to tension 4, knit one row, change back to tension 3 and knit 13 rows. Pick up cast on row (see diagram 6) and change tension to 6. Change row counter to 0. Knit 10 rows in 4 ply wool, increase 2 stitches both sides on tenth row. Change to 4 ply cotton, knit 10 rows and increase one stitch both sides. Knit in these stripes repeating increase of one stitch both sides every 10 rows until row 72 (68 stitches). Knitting should measure 20cm, including 2cm hem. Cast off.

Repeat for second sleeve.

Sleeves (method B): This method of knitting a sleeve is useful for making a very neat shoulder seam (see diagram 7).

Place back shoulder seam (wrong side facing you) and 5 stripes onto needles to the right of centre (see diagram 7). Place front shoulder seam and 5 stripes

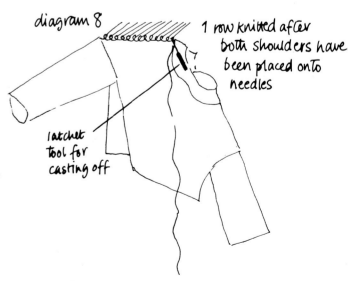

diagram 7
sleeve knitted from shoulder seam in place on 68 needles

armhole   central shoulder seam   armhole

back   front

onto needles left of centre, until there are 68 stitches (25cm) evenly cast on to the machine. With row counter at 0, tension 6, knit 10 rows using 4 ply wool. Decrease 2 stitches both sides. Continue knitting in stripes decreasing one stitch both sides every 10 rows until row 72 (52 stitches). Change to 2 ply cotton and to tension 3. Knit 13 rows. Change to tension 4 and knit one row. Change to tension 3 and knit another 13 rows. Pick up stitches from first row of hem onto needles and cast off.

Repeat for second sleeve.

To finish: Press knitting. When dry, place the stitches of front and back shoulder seams on the same needles (see diagram 8). Knit one row and cast off. This makes a better shoulder seam than when sewn up by hand. Sew side seams and arm seams by hand. To finish neck, sew inside collar seams first, then continue to outside.

diagram 8

1 row knitted after both shoulders have been placed onto needles

latchet tool for casting off

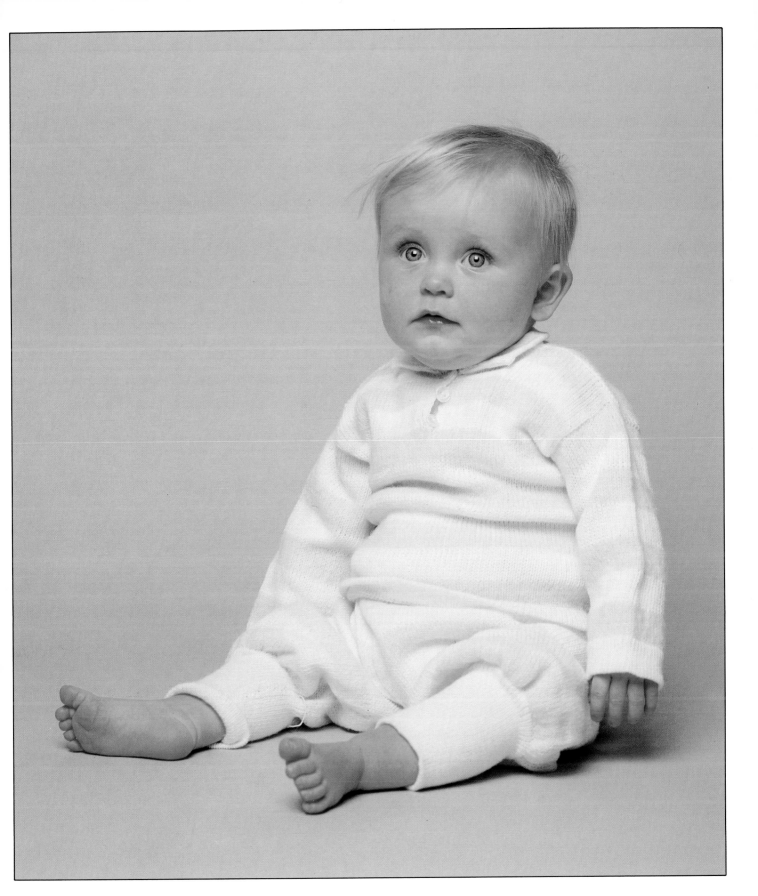

Variation 2: cabled cardigan

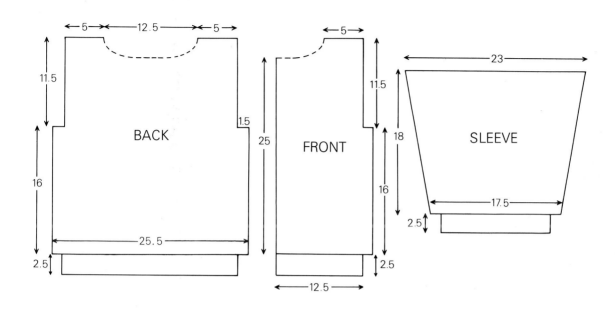

Materials
Knitted in Lister Motoravia 4 ply wool: 75gms fisher-man. 6 small pearl buttons.

Size
To fit baby aged up to 6 months (60cm).

Tension
Dial number 7
3.75 stitches = 1cm
5 rows = 1cm

Machines
Any domestic single-bed machine.

Back: Cast on 95 stitches (25.5cm), tension 7. Knit 12 rows (2.5cm) then drop every third stitch and pick up with latchet hook to form rib (see diagram 1b). Return row counter to 0. Continue knitting on all needles until row 80 for armhole shaping. Cast off 5 stitches (1.5cm) each side. Continue knitting until row 137. Cast off 18 stitches (5cm) both sides to form shoulders. Continue knitting neck section (rib) for 8 rows. Drop every third stitch to beginning of rib, pick up rib as for hem rib (see diagram 9) and cast off.

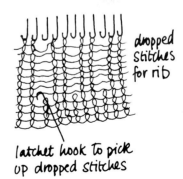

diagram 9 neck rib

dropped stitches for rib

latchet hook to pick up dropped stitches

Left front: Cast on 48 stitches (just over half to allow for front button placket). Form rib as for back. At row 12 return row counter to 0 and start cables over 4 needles (see diagram 10) leaving 4 stitches in between

17

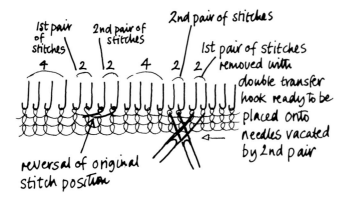

diagram 10   cable formation

1st pair
of
stitches

2nd pair of
stitches

2nd pair of stitches

1st pair of stitches
removed with
double transfer
hook ready to be
placed onto
needles vacated
by 2nd pair

4   2   2   4   2   2

reversal of original
stitch position

diagram 11

needles holding sleeve head and
half back and half front armhole

shoulder
seam

JJJJJJJJJJ   JJJJJJJJJ

left back armhole

left front
armhole

sleeve knitted from
half front and
back armhole

each cable. Continue cabling every 10 rows (rows 22, 32, 42, etc.) until row 80. Cast off 5 stitches (1.5cm) on left side for arm shaping. Continue cabling until row 125. Shape neck by holding out of action 2 needles every 2 rows so that 24 needles are held for neck shaping (row 137). Cast off 18 stitches (5cm) on left side for shoulder. Knit rib over 8 rows the same as for back neck. Cast off.

Right front: Knit the same as left front reversing shapings except in row 6 of rib from buttonhole 2 needles in from edge. Form next buttonhole row 12, then every 20 rows. Form last buttonhole second row of neck rib.

Sleeves: Cast on 65 stitches. Make rib over 12 rows. Increase 2 stitches both sides at row 10. Continue knitting and adding 1 stitch both sides every tenth row until by row 90 (18cm) there are 85 stitches. At row 90, onto the 85 needles holding the sleeve head, place the back left armhole (using 43 needles left of centre) and the front left armhole (using 42 needles right of centre). Cast off the two sets of stitches together (see diagram 11). This makes a better seam than sewing by hand.

Repeat for second sleeve.

To finish: Steam press, pin and sew together. Sew pearl buttons down left front.

Variation 3: intarsia cabled cardigan.

Materials
Knitted in Lister Motoravia 4 ply wool, 50gms fisherman; and Brockwell Wools 4 ply cotton, 50gms white. 8 small pearl buttons.

Size
To fit baby aged 3–6 months (60cm).

Tension
Dial number 7
3.37 stitches = 1cm (average of wool 3.25 stitches and cotton 3.5 stitches = 1 cm)
4.37 rows = 1cm (average of wool 4.5 rows and cotton 4.25 rows = 1cm)

Machines
Any single-bed machine with an intarsia carriage.

18

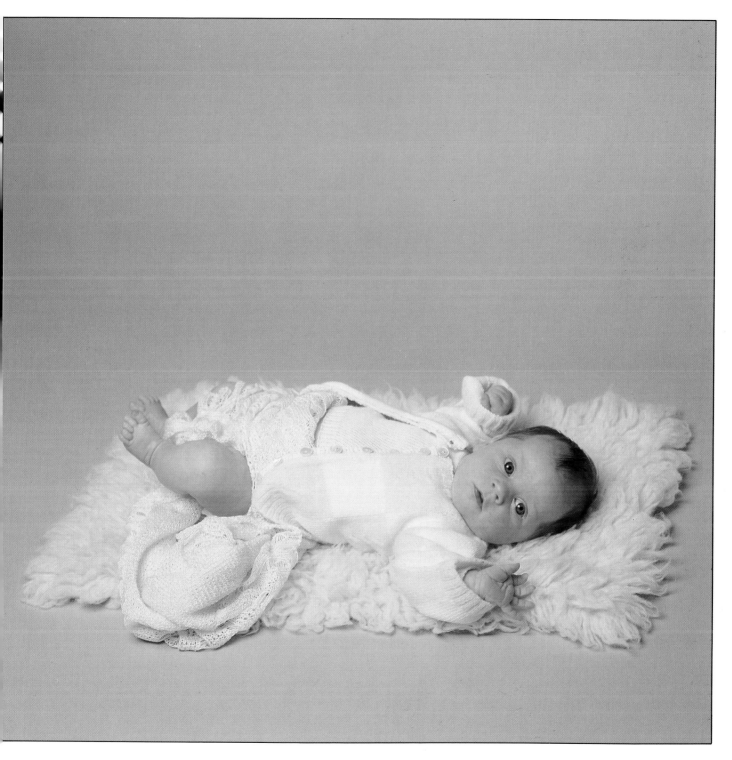

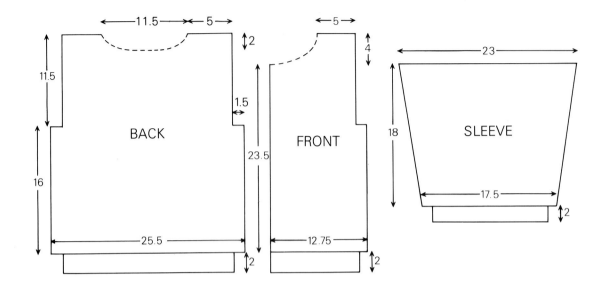

Back: Bring out 86 needles and in wool cast on 2 out of every 3 needles to form rib. On tension 7 knit 15 rows, pick up yarn in between pairs of needles to form rib stitches and place onto empty needles. Change row counter to 0. Change to intarsia carriage. Knit 28 rows in 21 stitches wool, 22 stitches cotton, 22 stitches wool, 21 stitches cotton. Reverse yarns and then reverse again at rows 56 and 84. Cable over 4 needles in centre of wool squares only (see diagram 12) every 8 rows. At row 70 shape armholes. Cast off 4 stitches carriage side (row 70) and 4 stitches carriage side (row 71). At row 72 decrease 1 stitch both sides and at row 73 decrease 1 stitch both sides. Continue knitting and shape neck at row 111. Push 37 needles left of centre forward out of knitting position. On right side, at row 111, push 12 more needles out on neck side and push 2 out at row 112. At row 113 push 2 out and 2 more out on row 115, then another 2 out at row 117. Cast off 17 stitches for shoulder seam on row 121. Leave stitches for neck out of action.

Repeat for left side from row 111.

Knit rib as for hem rib but in cotton onto shaped neck for 6 rows. Pick up stitches with latchet tool to form rib.

Right front: Tension 7, bring out 43 needles, cast on in wool 2 out of every 3 to form rib. Knit 15 rows, form rib as for back. Change row counter to 0, change to intarsia carriage. For right front: 22 stitches 4 ply, 21 stitches cotton, neck at left. Change yarns at rows 28, 56 and 84. Cable over 4 stitches in centre of wool squares only, every eighth row.

To shape armholes, at row 70 cast off 4 stitches, armhole side. At row 71 decrease 1 stitch and at row 72 decrease 1 stitch.

To shape neck, at row 103 push 6 needles forward out of action on the neck side. At row 104 push 7 needles out of action, at row 105 push 2 needles out of action and at row 107 push 2 needles out of action, 2 more on row 109 and 1 more on row 115.

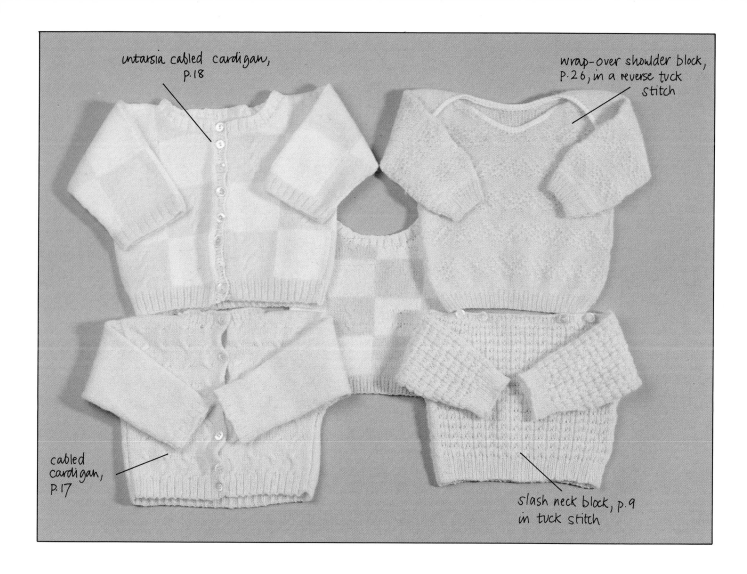

intarsia cabled cardigan, p.18

wrap-over shoulder block, p.26, in a reverse tuck stitch

cabled cardigan, p.17

slash neck block, p.9 in tuck stitch

Cast off remaining 17 stitches at row 121. Knit rib as for back in cotton.

Left front: Knit rib as for right front. Change row counter to 0, change to intarsia carriage. 21 stitches wool, 22 stitches cotton, neck at right. Repeat as for right front reversing shapings.

Sleeves: Pick up 78 stitches onto the machine (39 from the front armhole and 39 from the back armhole). Row counter at 0, tension 7, using intarsia carriage.

Right sleeve: 18 stitches wool, 21 stitches cotton, 21 stitches wool, 18 stitches cotton. Reverse yarns at row 5 and again at row 37. Decrease 1 stitch both sides fully fashioned at rows, 5, 13, 20, 27, 34, 41, 48, 55, 62. At row 78 change to normal carriage, knit 10 rows. Drop every third stitch, make rib using latchet hook, cast off.

Left sleeve: 21 stitches wool, 18 stitches cotton, 18 stitches wool, 21 stitches cotton. Knit as for right sleeve.

Front button band: Place one side of centre front opening evenly onto 54 needles, knit 5 rows at tension 7 in wool. Drop every third stitch and pick up to make rib with latchet tool.

Front buttonhole band: Knit as for button band except make buttonholes by transferring stitches every sixth needle at row 3.

To finish: Press and sew seams. Sew pearl buttons to front button band.

21

3. RAGLAN SLEEVE BLOCK

Materials
Knitted in Brockwell Wools 2 ply white cotton: 50gms.
4 small pearl buttons. See photo, page 10.

Size
To fit baby aged up to 3 months (50cm).

Tension
Dial number 3
3.5 stitches = 1cm
5.25 rows = 1cm

Machines
Any domestic single-bed machine.

Back: Using 75 stitches (21.5cm) cast on pairs of stitches as for previous ribs (see diagram 1). Using tension 4, knit 14 rows. Pick up rib onto spare needles, change tension to 3 and row counter to 0. Knit 62 rows, increasing 1 stitch both sides evenly until there are 80 stitches in action at row 62.

Bring out of action on hold all needles left of centre. (It is necessary to knit each of the back halves separately for the back opening, see diagram 13.) Knit right side decreasing 1 stitch on the right on row 62 and thereafter every second row until row 101. (21 stitches decreased for raglan, leaving 19 for half neck back.)

diagram 13

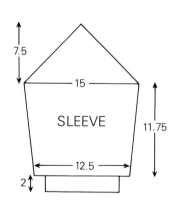

needles pushed out left side

To knit right side: needles knitting right of centre, right half of back

To knit left side: needles in knitting position

right side knitted needles pushed out of action for knitting on left

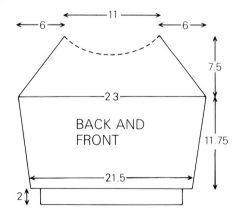

BACK AND FRONT

SLEEVE

22

Change to tension 4 and knit 10 rows. Drop every third stitch and pick up stitches to form rib. Cast off tightly.

Repeat for left half, decreasing left side and remembering to turn row counter back to 62.

Front: Using 75 stitches (21.5cm) cast on as for back. Knit rib (14 rows) as for back, change to tension 3 and pick up rib. Change row counter to 0. Knit 62 rows, increasing as for back until 80 needles are in action. Continue knitting, decreasing 1 stitch both sides on row 62, then every second row until row 90 (50 stitches).

To shape neck bring all needles left of centre into hold position. Continue knitting and decreasing for raglan and bring out of action 2 needles from centre on rows 91, 92, 93, 94, 95, 96, 97, 98 and 99 (see diagram 14). Hold 1 stitch on row 100 (19 stitches held for

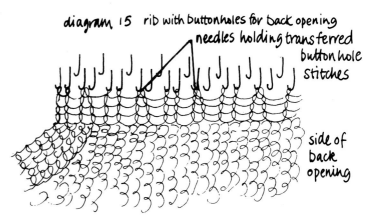

diagram 15 rib with buttonholes for back opening

needles holding transferred buttonhole stitches

side of back opening

diagram 14

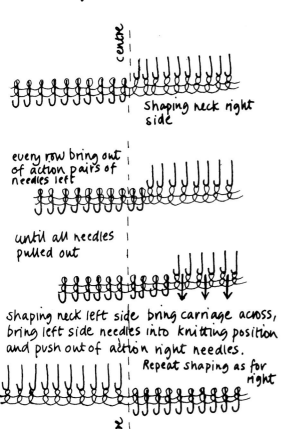

shaping neck right side

every row bring out of action pairs of needles left

until all needles pulled out

shaping neck left side bring carriage across, bring left side needles into knitting position and push out of action right needles.

Repeat shaping as for right

centre

centre

neck). Knit 1 row across so that both sides knit. Bring left side needles into knitting position, change row counter to 90 and repeat as for right side needles until 19 stitches held for neck. On the 38 stitches for neck, change to tension 4 and knit rib as before and cast off.

Sleeves: Bring out 44 needles, push out of action every third needle and with tension 4, knit 14 rows for rib. Make rib, change tension to 3 and row counter to 0.

Knit 62 rows increasing (from row 14) 1 stitch both sides every 16 rows until there are 52 stitches knitting. At row 62 start decreasing 1 stitch both sides fully fashioned. You need to decrease 26 stitches both sides over the next 39 rows so by row 101 there should be no stitches left.

Repeat for second sleeve.

Buttonhole band for back opening: Place left side of back opening onto 25 needles. Push out of action every third needle to form rib. With tension at 4, knit 3 rows. Transfer every sixth stitch to form 4 buttonholes (see diagram 15). Knit 4 more rows. Pick up stitches to form rib and cast off loosely.

To finish: Pin out and steam with damp cloth. When dry, pin together. Sew raglan sleeves to shoulder seams of body first, then sew side seams and arm seams. Finally, finish off loose ends of neck rib, and sew on pearl buttons.

Variation 1: wide high (polo) neck and cables.

Materials
Knitted in Lister Motoravia 4 ply wool, doubled: 125gms of fisherman.

Size
To fit baby 3–6 months (60cm).

Tension
Dial number 2.5
2.2 stitches = 1cm
2.2 rows = 1cm

Machines
Any domestic single-bed machine.

Back: Using 55 stitches (25cm) cast on alternate needles. With tension at 6, knit 14 rows (3.5cm). Make rib using latchet hook, placing new stitches onto empty needles. Knit one row. Make cable transfer with two pairs of stitches leaving 3 stitches between each cable (see diagram 16). Change tension dial to 2.5 and row counter to 0, continue knitting making cable transfers every 7 rows. (Change tension dial to 6 every seventh row to facilitate cable transfer.) After 26 rows (12cm)

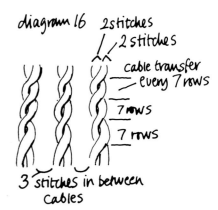

start decreasing fully fashioned and lose 13 stitches on alternate sides (26 stitches altogether) over 29 rows (13cm) to shoulder point. You should be left with 29 stitches. (Lose one stitch every row except for last 4 rows.) Drop every alternate stitch, push empty needles out of action, change tension dial to 6 and knit 16 rows. Form rib with latchet tool and cast off.

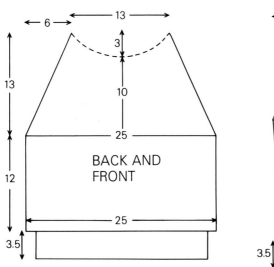

BACK AND FRONT

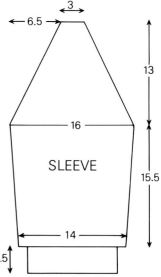

SLEEVE

24

Front: Knit as for back. On row 22 of knitting fully fashioned for raglan sleeves start neck shaping. For the right side, put all left side needles on hold. On row 22 hold 4 stitches right side, on row 24 hold 4 stitches, on row 26 hold 4 stitches, on row 28 hold 2 stitches. Repeat for left side from row 22 of fully fashioning for sleeve. Knit rib as for back on held neck stitches and cast off.

Sleeves: Cast on 30 stitches and with tension at 6, knit 14 rows (3.5cm) to form rib. Pick up rib with latchet tool. With row counter at 0 and tension at 2.5, knit 34 rows making one cable starting on row 2 in the centre of the sleeve as for back over two pairs of stitches. On every seventh row change to tension 6 to facilitate cable transfer. Increase 1 stitch on both sides on rows 12, 24 and 34 (36 stitches). Starting on row 35 decrease, fully fashioned, for raglan over 28 rows (1 stitch every row at alternate sides, 2 stitches last row). Cast off remaining 6 stitches.

To finish: Steam press, pin and sew side seams.

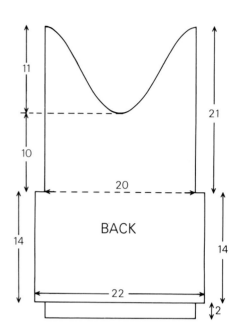

4. WRAP-OVER SHOULDER BLOCK

Materials
Knitted in Lister Motoravia 4 ply wool and Brockwell Wools 2 ply cotton. 100gms of fisherman wool, 25gms white cotton. See photo, page 10.

Size
Knitted to fit baby aged up to 3 months (50cm).

Tension
Dial number 6
3 stitches = 1cm
4.5 rows = 1cm

Machines
Any domestic single-bed machine.

Back: Using 66 needles (22cm) and tension 8, cast on alternate needles in wool. Knit 9 rows. Form rib with latchet hook. Change tension to 6 and row counter to 0. Knit 63 rows (14cm). Decrease 3 stitches both sides

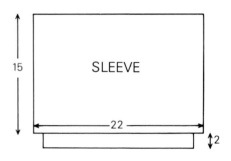

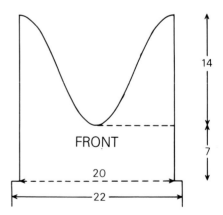

26

for armholes. Knit 45 more rows (10cm) to beginning of neck shaping. On row 108 push needles right of centre out of action. Hold 30 stitches over 50 rows: 1 stitch every alternate row until fortieth row (row 148), then every row until fiftieth row (row 158), see diagram 17. Repeat for right side of neck shaping.

Change to cotton for the neck edging and change tension dial to 2. Knit 5 rows. Knit 1 row at tension 3 and 5 more rows at tension 2. Pick up first row of edging. Cast off.

Front: Knit exactly as back until row 95 for neck shaping. Push needles left of centre out of action and hold 30 stitches over 63 rows (1 stitch every alternate row). Repeat for left side. Complete as for back.

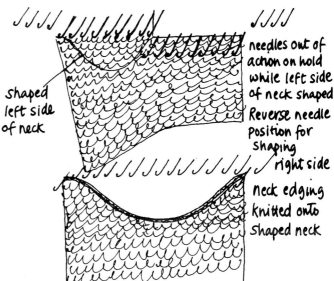

diagram 17 neck shaping

needles out of action on hold while left side of neck shaped

Reverse needle position for shaping right side

shaped left side of neck

neck edging knitted onto shaped neck

diagram 18

centre of sleeves and neck

sleeve

centre of overlap of back and front

front overlapped by back

sleeve

Sleeves: Using 66 needles (22cm) cast on alternate needles and with tension at 8 knit 9 rows. Make rib with latchet hook as for back. Return row counter to 0. Knit 67 rows (15cm). Cast off.

Repeat for second sleeve.

To finish: Steam press, pin and sew seams, centring sleeve head with centre of back, overlapping front to form wrap-over shoulder. (See diagram 18.)

27

5. LEGGINGS BLOCK

Materials

Knitted in Brockwell Wools 4 ply white cotton and Lister Motoravia 4 ply wool in fisherman. 65gms cotton, 65gms wool. 50cm of 2.5cm elastic.

Knitted in stripes to match block 2, variation 1 (pages 13–15). See photo, page 10.

Size

To fit baby aged 3–6 months (60cm).

Tension

Legs: dial number 6
    2.75 stitches = 1cm
    4 rows = 1cm
Cuffs: dial number 2 (single cotton)
    3.75 stitches = 1cm
    5 rows = 1cm

Machines

Any domestic single-bed machine.

Legs: Cast on 110 needles (40cm) in wool. With tension at 6, knit 60 rows in stripes (10 rows wool, 10 rows cotton). Decrease 1 stitch both sides on every alternate row until row 72 (96 stitches). Continue knitting for 58 rows in stripes until row 130.

To make waistband, change to cotton and to tension 2. Knit 15 rows, knit 1 row at tension 4 and knit another 15 rows at tension 2. Pick up first row of hem and cast off.

Repeat for second leg.

Ankle cuffs: Place onto machine cast on row of leg, placing 2 stitches onto every needle (55 needles in use), see diagram 19. Using cotton and tension 2, knit 40 rows. Knit 1 row at tension 4 and knit another 40 rows at tension 2.

Pick up first row of cuff and cast off.

Repeat for second ankle cuff.

To finish: Steam press and sew cuffs together. Then sew inside leg seams, centre front and centre back seams. Thread elastic through waistband and sew up hole in waistband.

Note: If you want to add feet you could sew up the

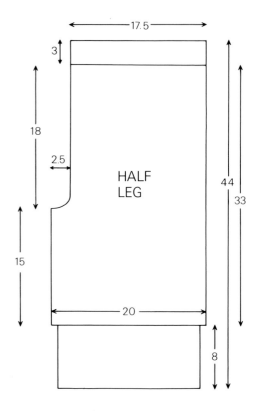

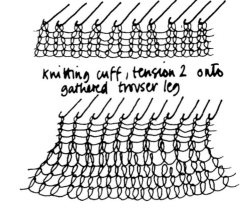

diagram 19
2 stitches on every needle
To produce gathering into trouser cuff

knitting cuff, tension 2 onto gathered trouser leg

ends of the ankle cuffs. For socks, moccasins, etc., please see chapter 7, page 106.

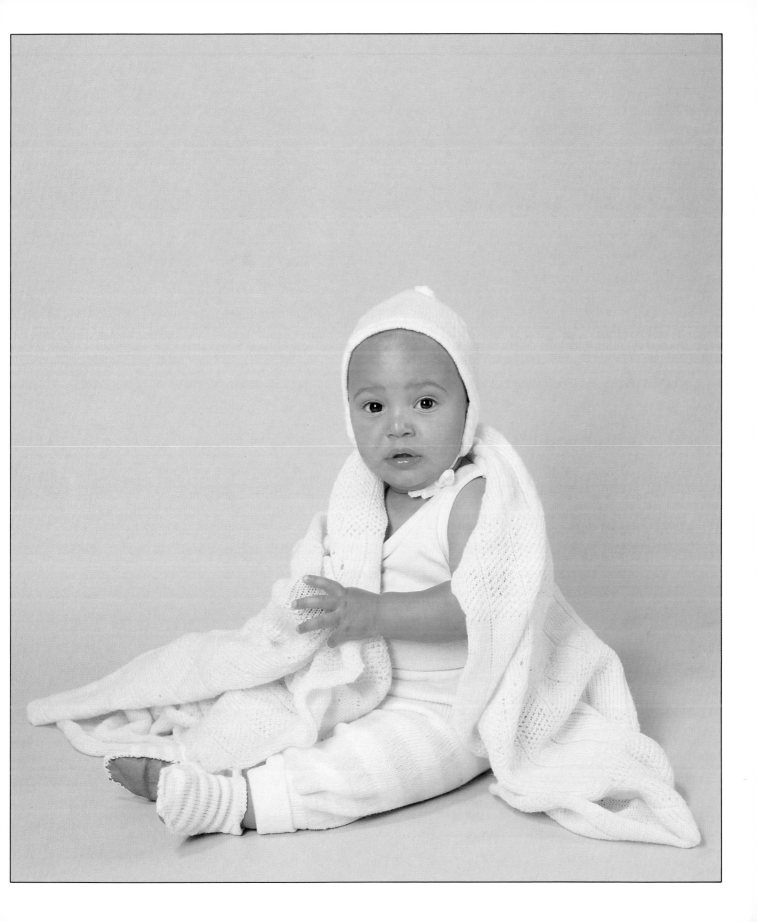

2 The Traditional Baby

Traditionally, babies are still dressed in white and pastel colours. Although this is becoming less common, and very unconventional babies can be observed in a remarkable diversity of colours and shapes, there are still plenty of traditional babies making a chapter for them essential.

Some of the 'baby blocks' already introduced can be adapted to suit the traditional baby. For example, the cardigan (page 17) will here be exaggeratedly large and will be knitted in white cotton with a pastel pattern. Also, the crew neck jersey (page 22) will be knitted in a Fair Isle pattern to make an invaluable baby bag. If a baby bag is attractive, the knowledge that the baby's undergarments are not well co-ordinated will be of little importance, unless, that is, the baby is exposed minus its lovely, warm bag.

The christening is where the traditional baby shines and a pattern is included for a knitted shawl; a vital garment for any traditionally-minded baby. However, it must not be too lacy in the middle as the baby will not only get very draughty but also gets its fingers and toes stuck in the holes: a sorry predicament for any baby.

The techniques and the patterns given here will be used again in subsequent chapters in different colour and stitch combinations. If your baby is not remotely traditional then please turn to another chapter where you are sure to find something more suitable.

TRADITIONAL CIRCULAR WOOLLEN SHAWL

Materials
Knitted in Lister Motoravia 4 ply wool: 600gms of fisherman; and Brockwell Wools undyed single mercerised cotton: 100gms.

Size
Large (see pattern for variations in size).

Tension
Dial number 9
Plain knitting 2.75 stitches = 1cm
                3.5 rows = 1cm
Lace stitch 2.6 stitches = 1cm
             2.5 rows = 1cm

The radius of each fully fashioned section in plain knitting measures 52cm (144 stitches). Because the lace sections are looser in construction the radius of these sections is, of course, longer. The full radius includes the unknitted circle in the centre which measures 24cm across at its widest point, so that total radius is 64cm. However, the 24cm of this central circle is lost in the gathering of the finished shawl.

Pattern punchcard in lace pattern (see diagram 20). Punch card before starting to knit.

Machines
Any domestic single-bed machine with punchcard facility.

The outer shaped sections: Cast on 144 stitches leaving out of action every tenth needle (16 needles out of action) (see diagrams 21 and 22). (If you want a smaller shawl cast on fewer stitches, perhaps only 100.) Knit 2 rows. Put carriage onto hold and leave it in this position throughout knitting. Place weights securely along needlebed. Beginning at the left edge, hold 81 stitches, knit 2 rows. Hold 85 stitches and knit 2 rows. Hold 94 stitches and knit 2 rows. Hold 130 stitches and knit 2 rows. Hold 112 stitches and knit 2 rows. Hold 121 stitches and knit 2 rows. Hold 130 stitches and knit 2 rows. Hold 139 stitches and knit 2 rows. (This should leave only 5 needles at the right side in knitting position.)

Push back into knitting position the last 9 held needles leaving 130 on hold, and knit 2 rows. Continue pushing back groups of 9 needles (the same previously put on hold) and knitting 2 rows until only 5 needles

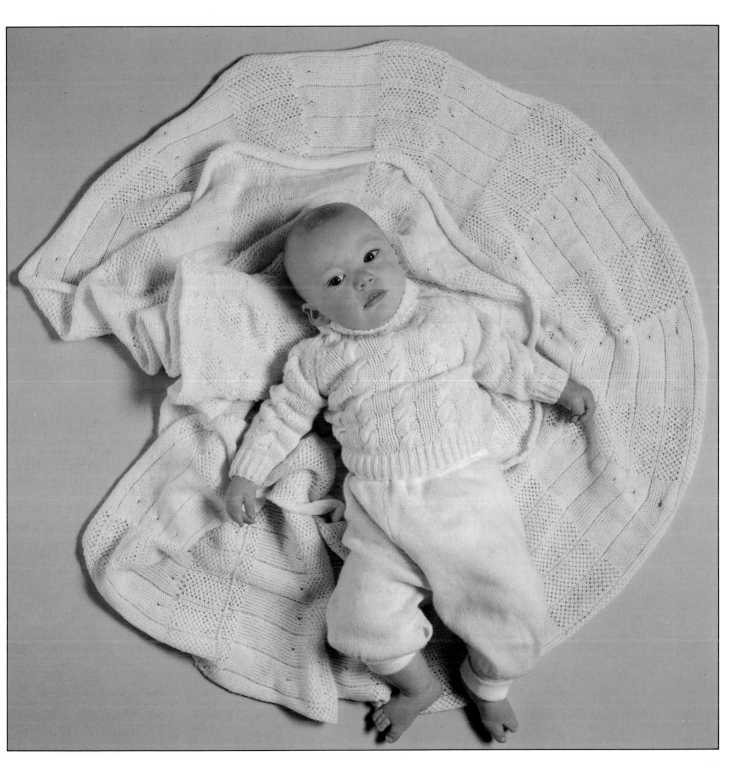

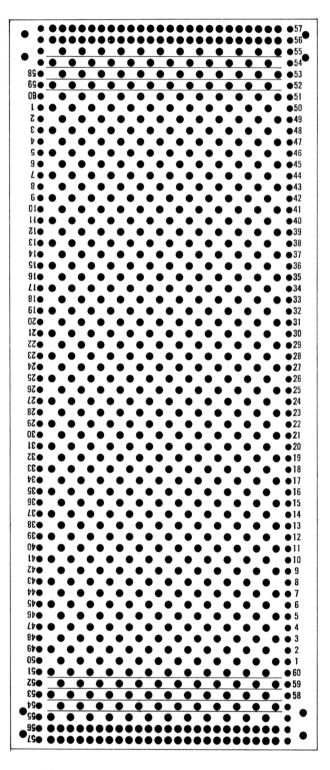

remain on hold on the left side. Push these into knitting position. Knit 2 rows.

Change row counter to 0, prepare carriage to knit lace using punchcard and thread cotton through second feeder. Knit 8 rows across the length of the needles in action. (If you want less gathering at the centre knit fewer rows here; perhaps 4 or 6.) Hold 5 needles from the left and knit 2 rows. Hold 9 more needles and knit 2 rows. Continue holding groups of 9 needles and knitting 2 rows until row 26 (leaving six groups of 9 needles on hold – 54 needles plus 5 at the far right).

Change row counter to 0, remove cotton and start ordinary knitting. Continue holding groups of 9 needles from where the six groups of 9 needles remain, until all the needles except the 5 at the far right are held. Begin pushing back into knitting position the groups of 9 needles until 15 groups have been pushed back and knitted and only 5 needles remain at the far left. Push these back, and knit 2 rows (row 46).

Change row counter to 0, prepare to knit lace using punchcard and thread cotton through second feeder. Knit 8 rows of lace before beginning shaping by holding needles. Repeat as in lace section above, until row 26.

Change row counter to 0, remove cotton and start ordinary knitting. Repeat as for knit rows until 46 rows have been knitted.

Repeat the lace section followed by a knit section until there are 21 lace sections and 21 knit sections (including the first one).

The last section will be lace. After the last row of the twenty-first lace section pick up the first row of the first knit section and cast off the two sets of stitches together.

If a smaller shawl is required, decide on the radius, cast on the appropriate number of stitches and, if less gathering is required, knit fewer rows (only 2 or 4 instead of 8 rows of lace knitting without holding). This will make the central circle area much smaller.

diagram 20

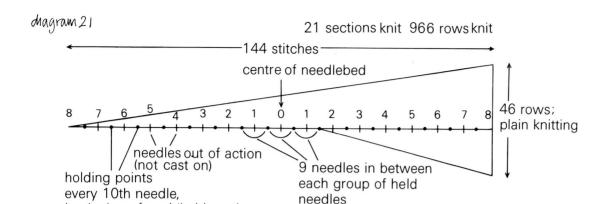

diagram 21

21 sections knit 966 rows knit

144 stitches

centre of needlebed

46 rows; plain knitting

8 7 6 5 4 3 2 1 0 1 2 3 4 5 6 7 8

needles out of action (not cast on)

holding points every 10th needle, beginning of each held section

9 needles in between each group of held needles

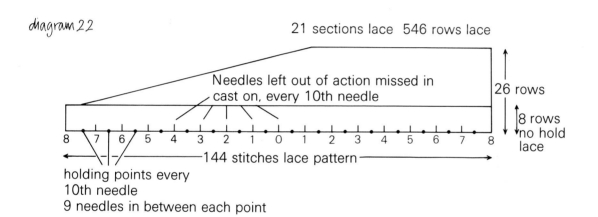

diagram 22

21 sections lace 546 rows lace

Needles left out of action missed in cast on, every 10th needle

26 rows

8 rows no hold lace

8 7 6 5 4 3 2 1 0 1 2 3 4 5 6 7 8

144 stitches lace pattern

holding points every 10th needle
9 needles in between each point

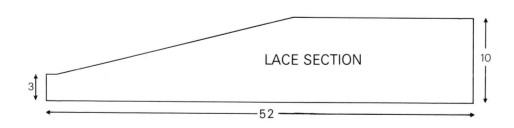

LACE SECTION

10

3

52

33

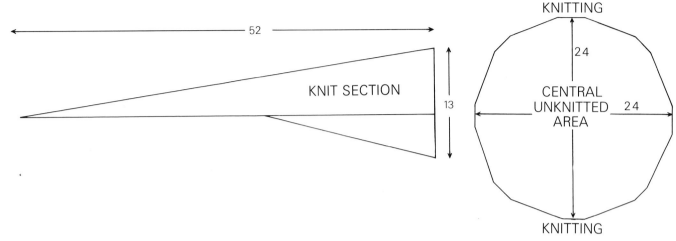

KNITTING

52

KNIT SECTION

13

CENTRAL
UNKNITTED
AREA

24

24

KNITTING

To finish: Without pulling out of shape, steam press each section to uncurl the edges. Using the mercerised cotton (doubled) run a thread evenly around the inside of the central circle. Draw the thread tight. Sew securely. Press again.

BABY BAG

Materials
Knitted in Lister Motoravia 4 ply wool: 250gms of fisherman. British Mohair Spinners 3 ply kid mohair: 25gms green, 25gms lilac, 25gms pink, 25gms yellow. Brockwell Wools 4 ply cotton, 200gms white.
A 56cm zip.

Size
To fit baby aged up to 9 months (70cm).

Tension
Dial number 6
3 stitches = 1cm
4.1 rows = 1cm
Pattern punchcard in Fair Isle pattern (see diagram 23). Punch card before starting to knit. This pattern is also effective knitted in one colour Fair Isle if the prospect of 6 colour changes, almost every row, is too daunting.

Machines
Any domestic single-bed machine with a punchcard facility.

Back: Cast on 124 stitches (41.5cm) in fisherman. With tension at 6, knit 2 rows. Begin patterning with punch-

ROW	FEEDER B
52-53-54	lilac
50-51	green
48-49	pink
46-47	empty
44-45	white cotton
43	lilac
41-42	white cotton
39-40	empty
37-38	white cotton
36	yellow
35	pink
34	green
33	lilac
32	green
31	pink
30	yellow
28-29	white cotton
26-27	empty
24-25	white cotton
23	green
21-22	white cotton
19-20	empty
17-18	pink
15-16	lilac
12-13-14	green
10-11	lilac
8-9	pink
6-7	empty
4-5	white cotton
3	yellow
1-2	white cotton
59-60	empty
57-58	pink
55-56	green

diagram 23   Feeder A = 4 ply wool

35

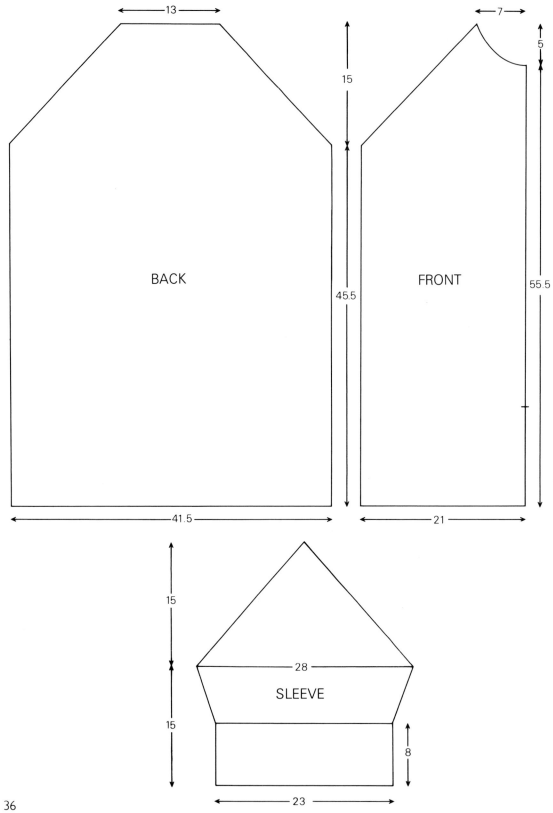

BACK

13

15

45.5

41.5

FRONT

7

5

55.5

21

SLEEVE

15

15

28

8

23

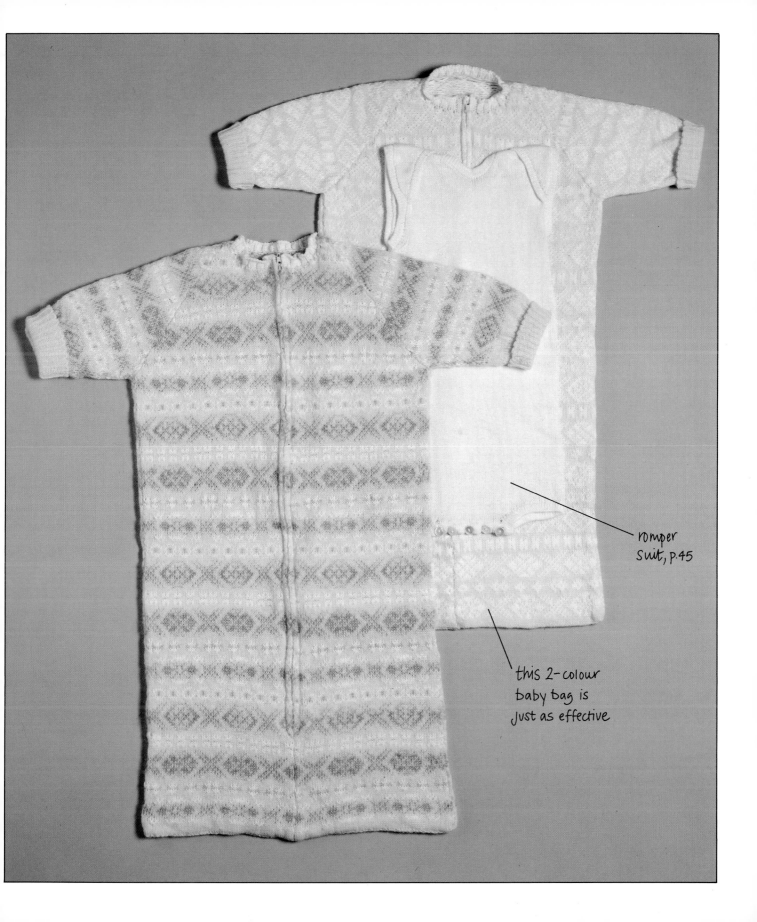

romper
suit, p.45

this 2-colour
baby bag is
just as effective

card row number on 27. Continue knitting, changing colours as shown (see diagram 23) until row 186. Begin decreasing on both sides: 2 stitches both sides every third row until row 248 (lose 42 stitches both sides leaving 40 stitches for back neck). Knit 6 rows, drop every third stitch and make rib with latchet tool (see diagram 24). Cast off.

Right front: Cast on 63 stitches (21cm) in fisherman. Knit 2 rows. Begin patterning with punchcard row number on 27. Continue knitting as for back until row 186. Decrease as for back until row 226. To shape neck, on row 227 begin bringing out needles into holding position. Continue to decrease for raglan as for back and bring out 6 needles from the centre (see diagram 25). On row 229 bring out 4 needles; on row

231, 3 needles; on row 233, 2 needles; on row 235, 2 needles; on row 237, 2 needles; on row 239, 1 needle; on row 241, 1 needle; on row 243, 1 needle and on row 248, 1 needle. Knit 6 rows on the 23 held stitches and form rib with latchet tool as for back. Cast off.

Left front: Repeat as for right front, reversing shapings.

Sleeves: Cast on 70 stitches (23cm) in fisherman. With tension at 6, knit 33 rows (8cm) leaving every third needle out of action. Form rib with latchet tool, placing formed stitches on empty needles. Start patterned knitting on row 34 (row number 7 of punchcard). Increase 1 stitch on both sides every fourth row until row 62 (84 stitches). At row 63 start decreasing for raglan. Decrease 1 stitch both sides every row for 3 rows, then knit 1 row with no decrease. Repeat until row 94. Knit 1 row with no decrease then 2 rows decreasing 1 stitch both sides. Repeat until row 122 when there should be no stitches left. If you find knitting Fair Isle too fiddly over 4 stitches, cast off when only 4 stitches remain (see diagram 26). This will not noticeably affect the pattern.

Repeat for second sleeve.

diagram 24

2 x 1 rib

latchet hook to form rib with dropped stitches

back raglan decreasing to neck

diagram 25 Shaping neck and decreasing raglan sleeve simultaneously

all stitches on hold while knitting right side

centre

6 stitches on hold right of centre

Left side

Right side

Beginning of neck shaping. Continue to decrease right side of raglan while shaping neck

diagram 26

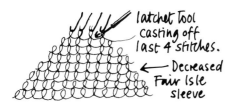

latchet tool
casting off
last 4 stitches.
← Decreased
Fair Isle
sleeve

To finish: Before steam pressing and sewing together, and depending on your patience, knot all the ends and cut or thread each loose end through the loops at the back. Or, use a sewing machine to zig-zag over the edges. To attach the zip, neatly turn a 0.25cm hem down the centre fronts. Pin in the zip from the beginning of the neck band, making sure that the front edges of the Fair Isle pattern match across the zip. Sew the centre front seam below the zip and then sew in the zip.

If you have been patient enough to knit this time-consuming baby bag the result is infinitely rewarding.

RAGLAN-SLEEVED FAIR ISLE SWEATER

Materials
Knitted in Brockwell Wools 3 ply white cotton and British Mohair Spinners 3 ply kid mohair in lilac. 40gms cotton, 40gms mohair. 4 small pearl buttons.

Size
To fit baby aged 3–6 months (60cm).

Tension
Dial number 6
3.1 stitches = 1cm
3.8 rows = 1cm
Pattern punchcard in Fair Isle pattern (see diagram 27).
Pattern block adapted from baby bag block (page 34).
Punch card before starting to knit.

diagram 27 – start card on punchcard
row 5 for back and front. start card on
row 60 for sleeves

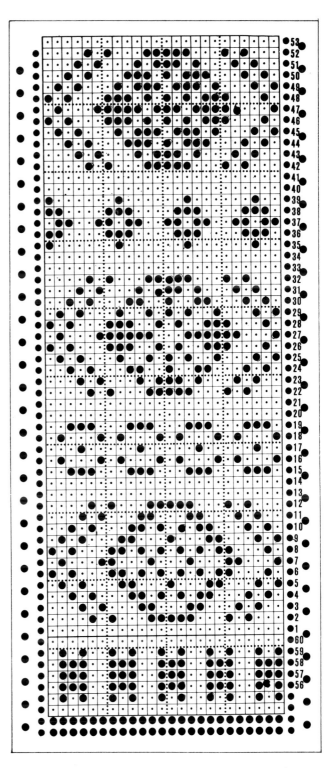

raglan-sleeved
Fair Isle sweater, p.39

capacious Fair Isle
cardigan, p.42

leggings, p.48

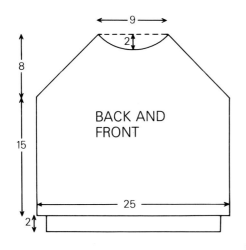

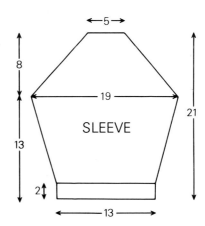

Machines

Any domestic single-bed machine with punchcard facility.

Back: Using cotton, cast on 78 stitches (25cm). With tension at 5, knit 10 rows, drop every third stitch and form rib with latchet tool. Change to tension 6. Thread mohair into feeder 2. Start punchcard at row 5. With row counter at 0, knit 57 rows in Fair Isle (15cm, excluding rib). Begin armhole by decreasing 1 stitch both sides every row for 4 rows (row 61). To make back opening, push all needles left of centre into hold position. (Note the row number on the punchcard (6) so you can turn back to correct row for other side.)

Continue knitting in Fair Isle decreasing 1 stitch every row until row 83. Knit 4 rows with no decrease. There should be 14 stitches remaining for neck. Knit 4 rows. Drop every third stitch and form rib with latchet tool. Cast off.

Turn punchcard back to number noted (6) and turn row counter back to row 61. Repeat decreasing for left side and repeat rib. Cast off.

Front: Cast on 78 stitches (25cm) in cotton. Knit as for back until 57 rows knitted in Fair Isle plus 10 rows rib, (6 rows total). Start armhole decreasing. Decrease 1 stitch both sides until row 83 (44 stitches). To shape neck, at row 83 push all needles left of centre into hold position plus 5 needles from right of centre (see diagram 25). Make a note of the row number on the punchcard (28). Continue decreasing 1 stitch every row simultaneously shaping neck by pushing 3 needles out

of action on rows 84, 85, 86 and 87. On row 88 there should be no stitches left unheld.

Repeat for left side from row 83 remembering to turn back the punchcard to row number 28.

Knit 4 rows and form rib as for back. Cast off.

Sleeves: Cast on 40 stitches (13cm). Knit 10 rows rib as for back. Thread mohair into feeder 2. Start punchcard at row 60, return row counter to 0. Knitting in Fair Isle increase 1 stitch both sides every fourth row until 24 (54 stitches). Increase 1 stitch both sides every fifth row until row 49. From row 50 decrease 1 stitch both sides every row until row 61. Then decrease 1 stitch both sides on every alternate row until row 79. Sleeve should measure 25cm. Knit 4 rows. Drop every third stitch and form rib with latchet tool. Cast off.

Repeat for second sleeve.

Back buttonhole band: Place left side of back opening, with right side of knitting facing you, onto 30 needles (see diagram 15). With tension at 6, knit 2 rows and make one buttonhole in the first 2 stitches down from the top of the neck edge. Make three more buttonholes, leaving 7 stitches between each. Knit 3 more rows. Drop every third stitch and form rib with latchet tool. Cast off.

To finish: Steam press into shape. Try to make sure that when you sew the garment together you match up the pattern across the body and sleeves. Sew 4 pearl buttons down the back opening.

41

CAPACIOUS FAIR ISLE CARDIGAN

Adapted from crew neck block (page 17)

Materials
Knitted in Brockwell Wools 4 ply white cotton (100gms), Rowan Yarns mercerised cotton in pink, yellow and mauve; and British Mohair Spinners 3 ply kid mohair in pink, yellow, and lilac: 25gms of each colour. 7 small pearl buttons. See photo, page 40.

Size
To fit baby aged 6–9 months (70cm and larger).

Tension
Dial number 5
3.3 stitches = 1cm
4.2 rows = 1cm

Pattern punchcard in Fair Isle pattern (see diagram 28, page 44). See diagram 28 for colour changes in pattern. Punch card before starting to knit.

Machines
Any domestic single-bed machine with a punchcard facility.

Back: Cast on 98 stitches (29.5cm) in white cotton. Knit 8 rows. Drop every alternate pair of stitches. Pick up dropped stitches with latchet tool to form rib. Turn punchcard to row 2 (do not thread second feeder until first patterning row as this produces unnecessary floats across the back of the knitting). To avoid this problem throughout the knitting it is worth familiarising yourself with punched pattern rows of the card.

Knit Fair Isle until row 75 (18cm including rib), changing or removing second yarn where necessary. (If in any doubt keep in second yarn.) For armhole, cast off

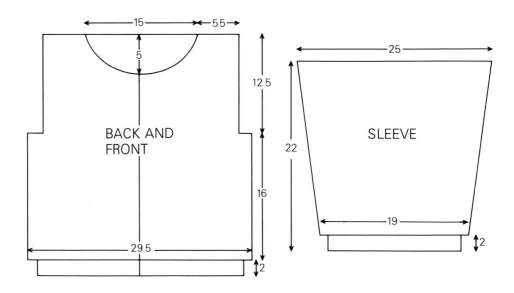

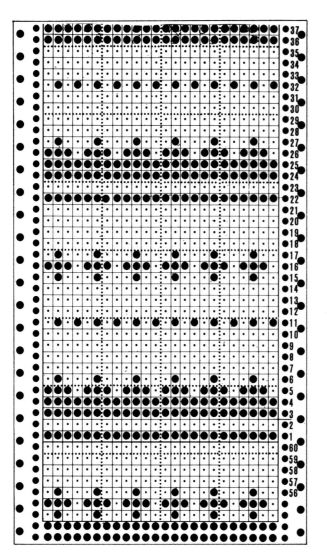

Row	Revolution 1	Revolution 2	Revolution 3
37	mauve cotton	yellow cotton	pink cotton
33-34-35-36	white		
29-30-31-32	yellow mohair	pink mohair	lilac mohair
28	white		
27	yellow cotton	pink cotton	mauve cotton
23-24-25-26	white		
20-21-22	pink cotton	mauve cotton	yellow cotton
17-18-19	white		
16	yellow cotton	pink cotton	mauve cotton
12-13-14-15	white		
8-9-10-11	pink mohair	lilac mohair	yellow mohair
7	white		
6	pink cotton	mauve cotton	yellow cotton
2-3-4-5	white		
59-60-1	yellow cotton	pink cotton	mauve cotton
56-57-58	white		

diagram 28

6 stitches at beginning of rows 76 and 77 (86 stitches). Continue knitting Fair Isle until row 129. Cast off 18 stitches both sides for shoulders (50 stitches remaining). Knit 8 rows. Make neck rib as for hem rib. Cast off.

Left front: Cast on 49 stitches in white cotton. Knit rib as for back. Start punchcard on row 2. Knit in Fair Isle until row 75. On row 76 cast off 6 stitches left side. Continue knitting until row 108. On neck side, push 8 needles into hold position on row 109. On row 111

hold 6 needles, on row 113 hold 3 needles, on row 115 hold 2 needles and then hold 1 needle on rows 117, 119, 121, 123, 125 and 127. On row 129 cast off 18 stitches for shoulder. Knit rib as for back on remaining 25 stitches. Front should measure 30.5cm.

Right front: Repeat as for left front, reversing shapings.

Sleeves: Cast on 62 stitches (19cm) in white cotton. Knit rib as for back. Turn punchcard to row 2. Have second yarn ready. Knit in Fair Isle pattern increasing 1 stitch both sides every eighth row until there are 82 stitches (row 88). Knit 4 rows in Fair Isle and cast off.

Repeat for second sleeve.

Front buttonhole band: Place centre front of cardigan onto 75 needles. At tension 6, knit 3 rows. Opposite every chevron-shaped Fair Isle and on neck band and hem rib, transfer 1 stitch to make buttonholes (7 in all). Knit 3 more rows. Drop every alternate pair of stitches and form rib with latchet tool. Cast off.

Front button band: Repeat as buttonhole band but do not make buttonholes.

To finish: Steam press. Sew in ends of loose yarn, pin and sew seams.

ROMPER SUIT (all-in-one vest) WITH LEG OPENING

Adapted from wrap-over shoulder block (page 26)

Materials
Knitted in Brockwell Wools 2 ply white cotton: 75gms.
5 flat buttons. See photo, page 37.

Size
To fit baby aged up to 6 months (60cm).

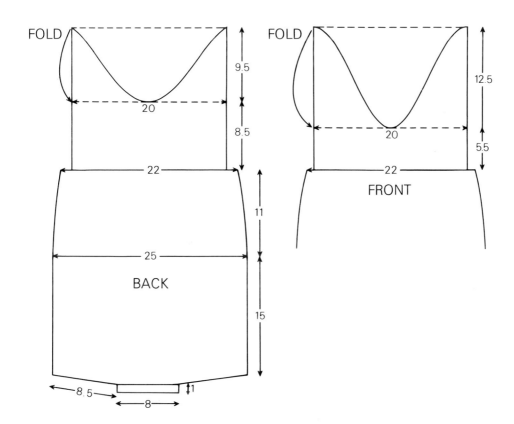

Tension
Dial number 2
3.75 stitches = 1cm
5.75 rows = 1cm

Machines
Any domestic single-bed machine.

Back: Cast on 30 stitches (8cm). Knit 7 rows at tension 2, 1 row at tension 3 and another 7 rows at tension 2. To make three buttonholes, transfer 1 stitch at needles 5, 15, 25 on row 3 and again on row 11 (see diagram 29). Pick up cast on row. Return row counter to 0. Knit,

casting on 3 stitches carriage side and increasing 1 stitch non-carriage side on every row until you have 94 stitches (4 stitches per row over 16 rows). Knit 86 rows. Over the next 64 rows (11cm) decrease 12 stitches (1 stitch both sides every 10 rows), making 82 stitches at row 166. Decrease 4 stitches carriage side on rows 167 and 168 for armhole and knit 46 rows to beginning of neck shaping (74 stitches on row 214).

Push all needles left of centre into holding position. Hold 3 stitches on rows 215, 217, 219, 221 and 223. Then hold 1 stitch on alternate rows, making sure that the yarn is passed under the last needle to prevent a hole from forming. Continue until 56 rows have been knitted and all needles are out of action. Knit 1 row in

diagram 29

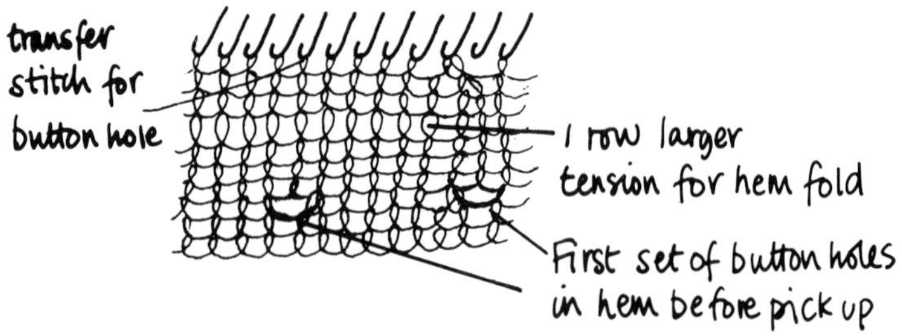

transfer stitch for button hole

1 row larger tension for hem fold

First set of button holes in hem before pick up

diagram 30
overlapping armholes placed onto 60 needles for armhole edging hem

< 30 needles >< 30 needles >
centre

6 needles   6 needles

front only

back only

back and front held on needlebed

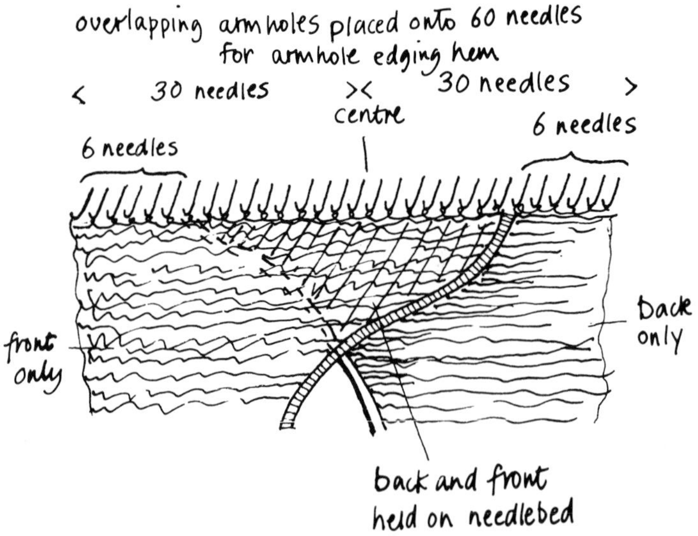

waste yarn to show where to pick up for hem. Push all needles on right side out of action. Repeat neck shaping for left side. Knit hem: 7 rows on tension 2, 1 row on tension 3 and 7 more rows on tension 2. Pick up first row of hem and last row of neck (ignoring waste yarn row) knit 1 row and cast off.

Front: Knit as for back until, after decreasing 4 stitches for armholes on both sides knit only 32 more rows then start neck shaping. Push all needles left of centre into holding position. Pushing 1 needle out at a time, knit 2 rows. Continue until row 270 when 72 rows have been knitted and all needles are out of action. Push all needles to the right out of action. Repeat neck

shaping for left side.
Knit hem as for back.

Armhole edging: Place overlapping shoulders to armholes both sides of centre onto 60 needles (see diagram 30), with overlap over central 48 needles. Knit hem as before.

Leg edging: Place back and front leg edges onto 30 needles (total 60) both sides of centre with side seam on centre needle (see diagram 31a). Knit hem as before, but make 2 extra buttonholes on back at join of hems (see diagram 31b).

To finish: Steam press. Sew seams and attach 5 buttons.

diagram 31a

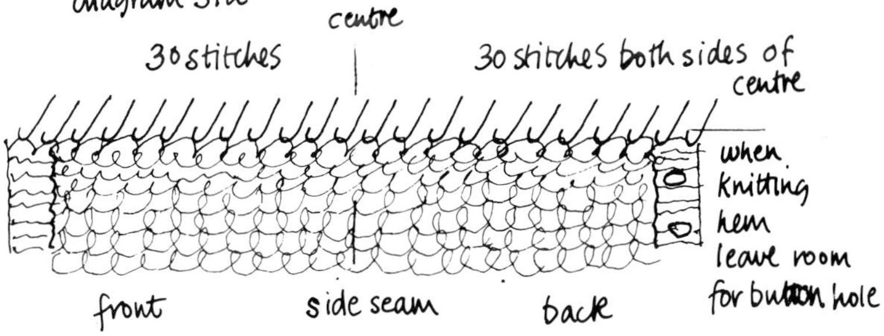

centre

30 stitches

30 stitches both sides of centre

when knitting hem leave room for button hole

front   side seam   back

Leg edging and positioning of button hole on seam edge

diagram 31b

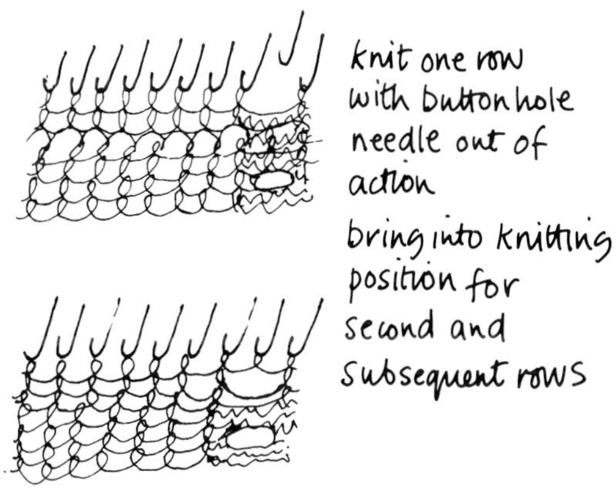

knit one row with button hole needle out of action

bring into knitting position for second and subsequent rows

Positioning of buttonholes on back at join of hems

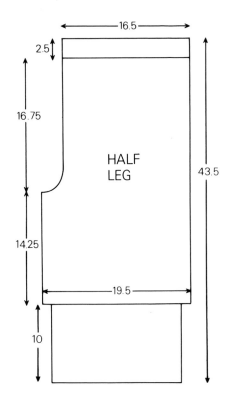

16.5

2.5

16.75

HALF
LEG

43.5

14.25

19.5

10

LEGGINGS

Adapted from the leggings block (page 28)

Materials
Knitted in Brockwell Wools 4 ply white cotton: 100gms.
50cm of 2.5cm elastic. See photo, page 40.

Size
To fit baby aged 3–6 months (50–60cm).

Tension
Legs: Dial number 3
      3.5 stitches = 1cm
      5.25 rows = 1cm
Cuffs: Dial number 2
      3.75 stitches = 1cm
      5 rows = 1cm

Machines
Any domestic single-bed machine.

Legs: Cast on 137 stitches (39cm). With tension at 3, knit 75 rows. Decrease 1 stitch both sides every row from row 75 to row 85 (leaves 115 stitches). Continue knitting until row 163 (31cm).
    To knit the waistband change tension to 2 and knit 15 rows.
    Knit 1 row at tension 4 and 15 more rows at tension 2. Pick up first row of hem and cast off.
    Repeat for second leg.

Ankle cuffs: Place cast on edge of leg onto machine putting 2 stitches onto every needle, 34 needles both sides of centre (68 needles in use). Knit 50 rows at tension 2, 1 row at tension 3 and 50 more rows at tension 2. Pick up first row of cuff and cast off.
    Repeat for second ankle cuff.

To finish: Steam press. Pin and sew up front and back seams. Sew up cuffs. Thread the elastic through waistband and sew up opening.

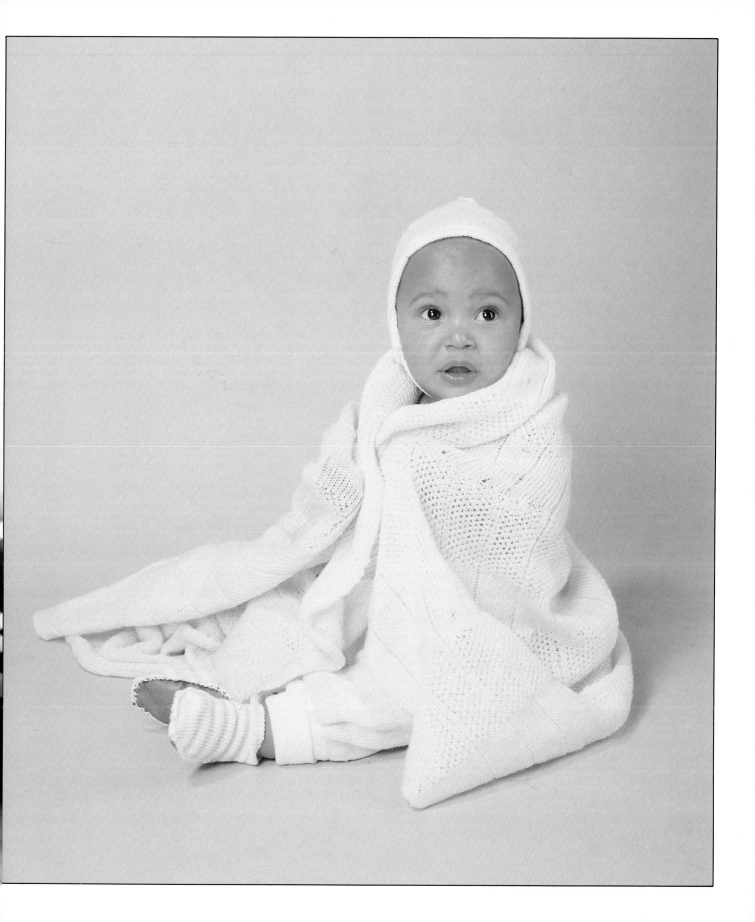

3 The Sporty Baby

The sporty baby, in contrast to the traditional 'seen-but-not heard' baby, is extrovert and noisy and suffers from insatiable curiosity at a frighteningly early age. These babies are never predictable, and, because of their inexhaustible energy, they have a talent for getting lost and for losing their clothes if the latter are not securely buttoned over their perpetually wriggling bodies. Their immense personal charm and precocious athleticism saves them from being monsters. Instead, most of them appear to be potential world class sports personalities.

To reflect the traits of the sporty baby (and to be practical) their clothes must be simple in construction, difficult to wriggle out of, as durable as possible and very bright – this will make the baby and its clothes far more difficult to lose!

The first garment is a striped football shirt, in contrasting yellow and navy, which is simple and conspicuous (see block 2 in chapter 1, page 13).

Then there's a navy jersey with a large collar and brightly striped ribs. It pulls on easily over the head but cannot be pulled off by its wearer. A pair of leggings completes this outfit. If their elasticated waist makes them too easy to lose then shoulder straps can be added for extra security; or for a foolproof solution the two garments can be knitted as one, making a romper suit (which will need buttons around the inside legs for access). Another version of this pattern is given in chapter 4, page 66.

The next outfit consists of a cabled intarsia jacket with a large collar and zip front. This can easily be elongated into a warm coat, with buttons rather than a zip, which should prevent the baby finding himself in the predicament of a hobbled camel! Under the zipped jacket baby can wear an intarsia cabled crew neck jersey buttoning down the back and a pair of red leggings with blue ribbed cuffs. (If extra security is needed apply the same solution as suggested for the navy outfit.)

Dressed in these clothes, sporty babies should neither lose their clothes, nor themselves.

STRIPED FOOTBALL JERSEY

Adapted from the crew neck block with set-in sleeves (page 13).

Materials
Knitted in Lister Motoravia 4 ply navy and yellow wool and Brockwell Wools 2 ply cotton in white. 65gms navy, 65gms yellow, 25gms white. 3 pearl buttons.

Size
To fit baby aged 9–12 months (80cm).

Tension
Dial number 7
2.75 stitches = 1cm
4 rows = 1cm

Machines
Any domestic single-bed machine.

Back: Cast on 74 stitches (27cm) in navy. Knit 10 rows at tension 7, 1 row at tension 9 (for hem fold) and 10 rows at tension 7. Pick up cast on row. Turn row counter to 0. Knit 10 rows yellow, 10 rows navy, until row counter is at 64. For armhole shaping decrease 1 stitch both sides for 6 rows until end of navy stripe on row 70. Continue knitting in stripes until row 100 (62 stitches), then begin decreasing for neck (see diagram 32, page 52). Hold all needles left of centre. Bring into holding position 2 stitches right of centre on rows 101, 102 and 103 and thereafter 1 stitch until row 114 when there will be 17 held stitches for right neck. Cast off right shoulder (14 stitches). With carriage on the left, repeat shaping for other side. Cast off left shoulder.

Back collar: See diagram 33. Change tension to 4 and thread yarn feed with single 2 ply white cotton. Knit 12 rows on 34 neck needles, change tension to 6 and knit 1 row. Change tension back to 4 and knit 12 more rows. Pick up first row of collar, knit 1 row and cast off.

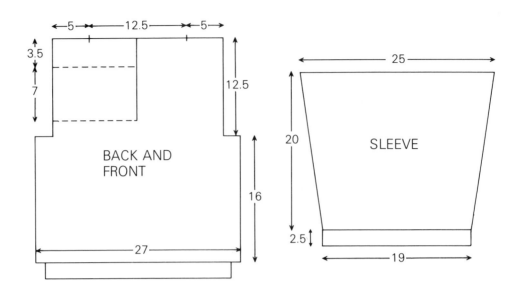

BACK AND FRONT

SLEEVE

diagram 32 Holding for back neck shaping

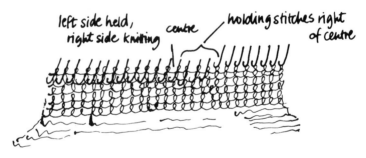

left side held,
right side knitting

centre

holding stitches right
of centre

diagram 33

shoulder cast off

neck on held needles ready to knit
white collar

shoulder cast off

shaped
stripes
at shoulder
and neck

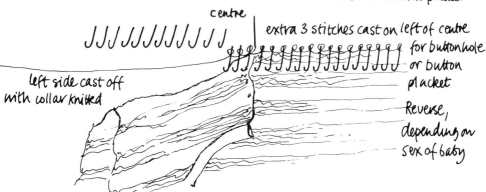

diagram 34 Casting on extra stitches left (or right) of centre for button or buttonhole placket

centre

extra 3 stitches cast on left of centre for buttonhole or button placket

left side cast off with collar knitted

Reverse, depending on sex of baby

Front: Repeat as for back until row 80 (20cm). Push all needles left of centre into holding position. Knit right side until row 100 and then begin neck shaping as for back. Cast off shoulder on row 114. Knit right front collar in white cotton as for back. Cast off.

To knit left side, turn row counter back to row 80. Cast on 3 stitches right of centre for buttonhole placket (diagram 34 shows reverse, depending on baby's sex). Make buttonholes (2 stitches from the edge) on rows 82, 94 and 100. On row 100 begin neck shaping as for right side, except hold the 3 extra stitches right of centre on row 101 as well. Knit collar as for right side (having cast off the extra 3 stitches on row 114).

Sleeves: Place armhole seams of back and front on both sides of centre with yellow armhole stripes on 6 needles each and the remaining 8 stripes on 7 needles per stripe. Total of 68 needles (25cm). With tension at 7 and starting with yellow, knit stripes every 10 rows decreasing 1 stitch both sides every 10 rows until there are 52 stitches left (80 rows). At row 80 knit 10 rows in navy, 1 row at tension 9, and 10 more rows at tension 7. Pick up first navy row, knit one row and cast off.

Repeat for second sleeve.

To finish: Pin and steam press. Pin so that stripes match. Sew together edge to edge using the appropriate colour for each stripe. Sew on 3 pearl buttons opposite buttonholes.

CHUNKY KNIT JERSEY WITH BIG COLLAR

Materials

Knitted in Lister Motoravia double knitting wool: 175gms navy, 25gms yellow, 25gms red, 25gms blue.

Size

To fit baby aged 12–18 months (80–90cm).

Tension

Dial number 4
1.75 stitches = 1cm
2.25 rows = 1cm

Machines

Any domestic chunky machine of 8 or 9mm gauge. If using an ordinary standard 4 or 5mm gauge machine then use 4 ply wool.

Back: Cast on 54 stitches (31cm). With tension on 1, knit 2 rows in navy, 1 row in red, 1 row in yellow and 1 row in blue. Knit 4 rows in navy, 1 row in red, 1 row in yellow, 1 row in blue and then 4 rows in navy. Drop alternate pairs of stitches and form rib with latchet tool. Knit 1 row in navy. Reverse each stitch so there will be one row of pearl before the main body of the jersey. This provides an interesting detail on the garment.

Return row counter to 0. Knit 45 rows, increasing 1 stitch both sides on rows 20 and 30. On row 45 cast on 26 stitches on the carriage side and knit 1 row. On row 46, cast on 26 stitches on carriage side. Knit 22 more rows. Cast off.

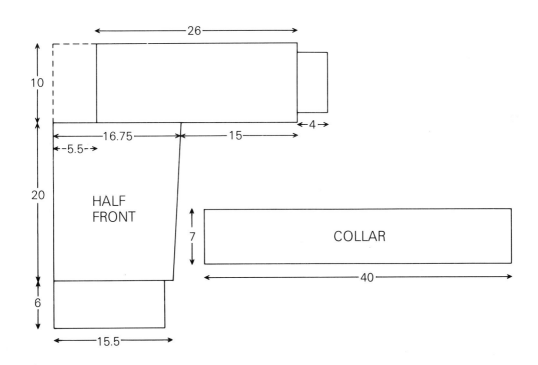

Front: Knit as for back until row 45. With carriage at the right cast on 26 stitches, push out into holding position all those needles left of centre, plus 10 needles right of centre. Knit 22 rows on these 45 stitches. Cast off right side shoulder seam. Transfer carriage to left side. Push into knitting position all needles left of centre leaving the 10 nearest the centre on hold. (These 20 central needles are held for neck.) Knit 1 row and with

carriage on the left cast on 26 stitches. Knit 22 rows. Cast off left side 45 stitches for shoulder seam. Cast off central 20 stitches of neck.

Rib for sleeve: With wrong side facing, place cuff of sleeve onto machine over 24 stitches (see diagram 35). With tension at 1, knit 2 rows in navy, 1 row in blue, 1 row in yellow and 1 row in red. Knit 4 rows in navy, 1 row in blue, 1 row in yellow, 1 row in red and 1 row in navy. Drop alternate pairs of stitches back to the second navy row, pick up stitches and form rib with latchet tool. Cast off.

Repeat for second sleeve.

Collar: Cast on 110 stitches. With tension at 1, knit 20 rows in navy, 1 row in blue, 1 row in yellow, 1 row in red and 1 row in navy. Drop alternate pairs of stitches and form rib with latchet tool. Cast off.

To attach collar to jersey, starting at the centre back, pin together with wrong sides facing. Sew together edge to edge (see diagram 36).

To finish: Steam press and sew seams.

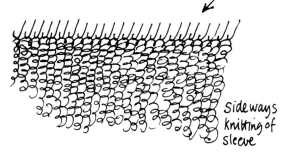

diagram 35 Knitting sleeve cuff rib
Place edge of sleeve onto 24 needles

Sideways knitting of sleeve

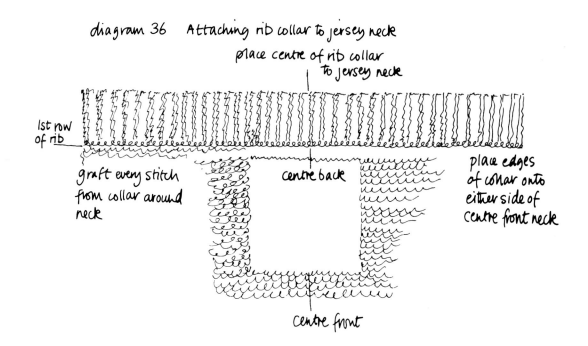

diagram 36 Attaching rib collar to jersey neck

place centre of rib collar to jersey neck

1st row of rib

graft every stitch from collar around neck

centre back

place edges of collar onto either side of centre front neck

centre front

57

LEGGINGS WITH RIBBED CUFF

Adapted from the leggings block, page 28.

Materials
Knitted in Lister Motoravia 4 ply navy wool: 250gms. 58cm of 2cm elastic. See photos, pages 53, 54.

Size
To fit baby aged 12–18 months (80–90cm).

Tension
Dial number 7
3 stitches = 1cm
4 rows = 1cm

Machines
Any domestic single-bed machine.

Legs: Cast on 138 stitches (46cm). With tension at 7, knit 84 rows. Decrease 1 stitch both sides for 7 rows. Knit until row 172 then add a fine, contrasting waste yarn for 1 row (so that you can see the row to pick up for the waistband). Knit 8 rows, change tension to 9 and knit 1 row.

Return tension to 7 and knit 8 more rows. Pick up first marked row of waistband and cast off. Remove waste yarn.

Repeat for second leg.

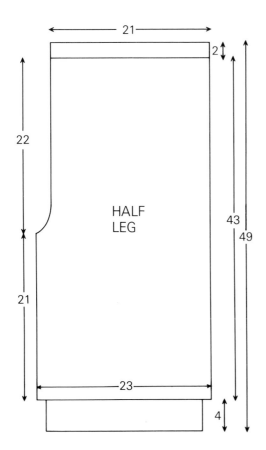

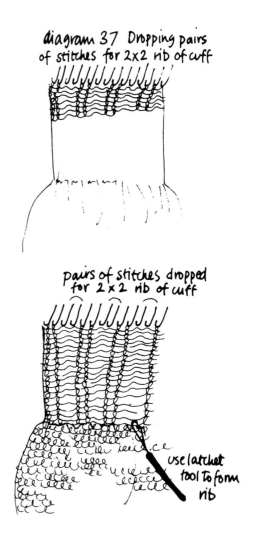

diagram 37 Dropping pairs of stitches for 2x2 rib of cuff

pairs of stitches dropped for 2 x 2 rib of cuff

use latchet tool to form rib

Cuffs: Place 2 stitches of cast on row of leg onto every one needle of 69 needles (23cm). With tension at 6 (in order to make rib tight) knit 16 rows.

Drop alternate pairs of stitches and pick them up with the latchet tool to form rib (see diagram 37).

Repeat for second cuff.

To finish: Pin flat and steam press. When pinning legs together ensure that the crotch seams are matched on both legs.

Starting with the leg seams, sew together. Thread waistband with elastic and complete sewing up.

CABLED INTARSIA JACKET
WITH ZIP FRONT

Adapted from the crew neck block with set-in sleeves, page 13.

Materials

Knitted in Lister Motoravia double knitting wool in yellow, blue and red, and Lister Richmond double knitting wool in domino. 35gms yellow, 35gms blue, 35gms red, 75gms domino. One 36cm open-ended zip.

Size

To fit baby aged 12–18 months (80–90cm).

Tension

Dial number 4
1.5 stitches = 1 cm
2.5 rows = 1 cm

Machines

Any domestic 8 or 9mm gauge chunky machine with an intarsia carriage.

Back: Cast on 48 stitches (32cm) in domino. With tension at 1, knit 10 rows. Drop alternate pairs of stitches, pick up stitches with latchet tool to form rib. Change tension to 4 and row counter to 0. Using an intarsia carriage knit in coloured squares: 12 stitches for each square, 18 rows deep. For sequence of colours see diagram 38, from right to left: red, blue, yellow, domino. Make a cable over 4 stitches in centre of blue

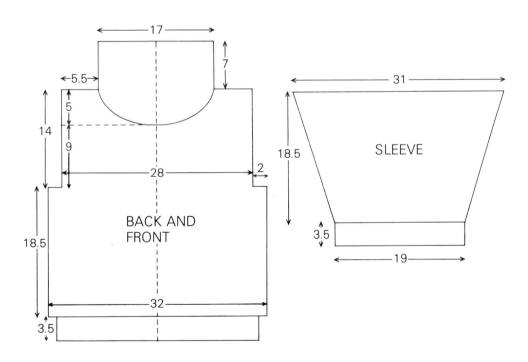

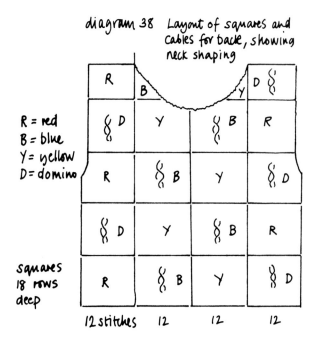

diagram 38 Layout of squares and cables for back, showing neck shaping

R = red
B = blue
Y = yellow
D = domino

squares 18 rows deep

12 stitches   12   12   12

diagram 39 Layout of squares and cables for front, showing neck shaping

squares 18 rows deep

12 stitches   12   12   12

squares on rows 4, 8 and 14. On row 18 change colour sequence to domino, yellow, blue, red and make a cable in the centre 4 needles of the domino and blue squares. After another 18 rows, change sequence to red, blue, yellow, domino with the cable in the centre of the blue and domino squares. At row 46 cast off 3 stitches both sides for armhole shaping (42 stitches left).

Continue changing coloured squares (see diagram 38) until row 68 to start of neck shaping. Push out of action all needles left of centre. Hold 2 stitches right of centre on row 68 then 1 stitch every row until row 80 (leaving 8 stitches for shoulder). Cast off shoulder at row 80. Take carriage to left side and leave 13 neck stitches on hold. Repeat as for right side, casting off shoulder after neck shaping. On remaining 26 needles and with tension at 3, knit 16 rows in domino. Drop alternate stitches and form rib with latchet tool. Cast off.

Right front: Cast on 24 stitches (16cm) in domino. With tension at 1, knit 10 rows. Drop alternate pairs of stitches and form rib with latchet tool. Change tension to 4 and row counter to 0. Using intarsia carriage knit coloured squares as for back starting from right to left with yellow, domino (see diagram 39). Cable as for back in yellow square. On row 18 change sequence to domino, blue and place cable in blue square. After another 18 rows change sequence to red, domino and place cable in red square. At row 46 cast off 3 stitches for armhole shaping. Continue until row 68 and start neck shaping. Beginning at the right side, hold 2 stitches on row 68 then 1 stitch every row until row 80 (leaving 8 stitches for shoulder). Cast off 8 shoulder stitches. On remaining 13 neck stitches knit 16 rows in domino with tension at 3. Drop alternate stitches, and form rib with latchet tool.

Left front: Repeat as for right front reversing square colours, armhole and neck shapings.

Sleeves: With wrong sides facing, place back left armhole over 23 needles right of centre. Place front right armhole over 23 needles left of centre (46 needles in all) (see diagram 40, page 62). Shoulder seams should be at the centre. Knit the sleeves so the two central squares have 12 needles each and the two outside squares 11 needles each. Knit squares for sleeve onto cast on armholes in sequence as follows.

Right sleeve: Decrease 1 stitch both sides every 5 rows leaving 28 stitches on row 46. Sequence starts blue,

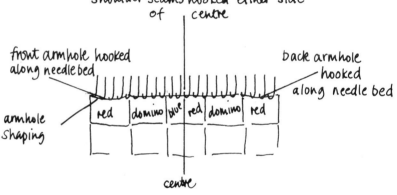

diagram 40 To knit right sleeve from armhole hooked along needle bed
shoulder seams hooked either side of centre

Back armhole hooked along needle bed

Front armhole hooked along needle bed

armhole shaping

| domino | red | domino | yellow | domino |

centre

diagram 41 To knit left sleeve from armholes hooked along needlebed
shoulder seams hooked either side of centre

front armhole hooked along needle bed

back armhole hooked along needle bed

armhole shaping

| red | domino | blue | red | domino | red |

centre

domino, blue, domino, 18 rows with cable in blue squares. Change sequence to domino, yellow, domino, yellow with cable in yellow squares. Change sequence to red, domino, red, domino with cable in red squares. Change tension to 1, knit 10 rows in domino. Drop alternate stitches and form rib with latchet tool. Cast off.

Left sleeve: Repeat as for right sleeve changing colour sequence only (see diagram 41). First row of squares: domino, yellow, domino, yellow with cable in yellow squares. Second row of squares: red, domino, red, domino with cable in red squares. Third row of squares: domino, blue, domino, blue with cable in blue squares. Knit rib as for right sleeve. Cast off.

To finish: Steam press gently. Carefully matching squares and using the appropriate colours sew seams edge to edge. Attach open-ended zip to fronts of jacket, preferably using a zig-zag stitch on a sewing machine.

INTARSIA CABLED JERSEY WITH BACK OPENING

Adapted from the crew neck block with set-in sleeves, page 13.

Materials
Knitted in Lister Motoravia 4 ply wool: 30gms turquoise, 30gms blue, 30gms red, 30gms yellow. 2 buttons. See photo, page 61.

62

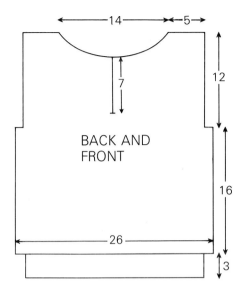

BACK AND FRONT

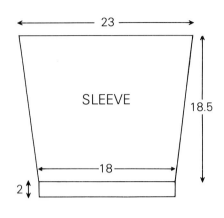

SLEEVE

Size
To fit baby aged 6–9 months (70cm).

Tension
Dial number 7
2.75 stitches = 1 cm
4.25 rows = 1 cm

Machines
Any domestic single-bed machine with an intarsia carriage.

Back: Cast on 72 stitches (26cm) in blue leaving every third needle out of action. With tension at 6, knit 15 rows. Pick up stitches with latchet tool to form rib. Return row counter to 0 and tension to 7. Using intarsia carriage knit in squares of 18 stitches of 30 rows. For squares' sequence see diagram 42, page 64. Change colour sequence of squares on rows 30, 60 and 90. Cable over 4 stitches on rows 9, 20, 39, 50, 69, 80, 99, 110. For armhole shaping decrease 2 stitches at the carriage side on rows 66 and 67. Decrease 1 stitch both sides on row 68. Knit until row 90.

For back neck opening leave centre squares unjoined at row 90. On row 111 push 11 stitches both sides of centre into hold position. Push 1 needle out of action every row, both sides, until row 119. On row 119, on these 28 remaining unheld needles cast off shoulders (14 stitches each shoulder).

With tension at 6, knit half neck rib on 19 stitches. Knit 6 rows, drop every third stitch and make rib with latchet tool. Cast off. Repeat for second half of neck rib.

Front: For sequence of square colours and cables see diagram 43. Knit as back (but do not separate centre squares at row 90) until neck shaping on row 109. Leave 10 needles both sides of centre on hold and push 1 needle out of action both sides every row, until row 119 (38 stitches on hold). Cast off shoulders (14 stitches each shoulder). With tension 6 knit neck rib as for back over 6 rows. Drop every third stitch and form rib with latchet tool. Cast off.

Sleeves: Place front and back armholes onto 64 needles both sides of centre with shoulder seam at centre. Squares for sleeve will be 14 stitches, 18 stitches, 14 stitches, 18 stitches (see diagram 44 for colour sequence). With row counter at 0 and tension at 7, knit 6 rows in the four colours. Change colour sequence of squares to red, turquoise, yellow, turquoise (see dia-

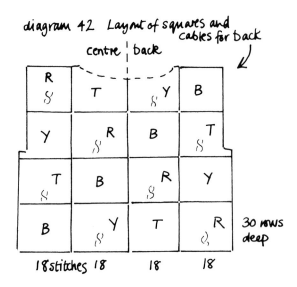

diagram 42 Layout of squares and cables for back

centre | back

R δ	T	Y δ	B
Y	R δ	B	T δ
T δ	B	R δ	Y
B	Y δ	T	R δ

30 rows deep

18 stitches 18   18   18

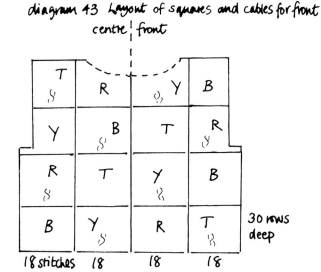

diagram 43 Layout of squares and cables for front

centre | front

T δ	R	Y δ	B
Y	B δ	T	R δ
R δ	T	Y δ	B
B	Y δ	R	T δ

30 rows deep

18 stitches 18   18   18

T = turquoise
R = red
Y = yellow
B = blue

gram 44). Decrease 1 stitch both sides on row 5. Change colours again at row 30 and row 60. Decrease 1 stitch both sides on rows 15, 24, 34, 44, 55 and 65 (leaves 50 stitches). At row 78 change tension to 6, knit 10 rows in blue. Drop every third stitch and form rib with latchet tool. Cast off.

Back opening: Pick up 21 stitches over 1 square and knit 4 rows at tension 6. Make 2 buttonholes on second row at stitches 9 and 19. Drop every third stitch and form rib with latchet tool. Cast off.

Repeat for other side of neck opening but do not make buttonholes.

To finish: Pin and steam press. Sew together carefully, with appropriate yarn colours, making sure that all squares match across seams.

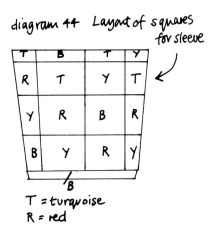

diagram 44 Layout of squares for sleeve

T	B	T	Y
R	T	Y	T
Y	R	B	R
B	Y	R	Y

B

T = turquoise
R = red
Y = yellow
B = blue

64

LEGGINGS WITH CONTRASTING RIBBED CUFFS AND BRACES

Adapted from the leggings block, page 28.

Materials
Knitted in Lister Motoravia 4 ply wool: 17gms red, 25gms blue. 4 pearl buttons. 56cm of 2cm elastic.

Size
To fit baby aged 6–9 months (70cm).

Tension
Dial number 7
3 stitches = 1cm
4 rows = 1cm

Machines
Any domestic single-bed machine for leggings, with a ribber attachment for braces. Or any double-bed machine for the braces.

Legs: Cast on 120 stitches (40cm) in red. With tension at 7, knit 60 rows. Decrease 1 stitch every row until row 74 (106 stitches). Knit until row 140 (35cm) and then add a fine, contrasting waste yarn for 1 row (so you can see which row to pick up for the waistband). Knit 10 rows, change tension to 9 and knit 1 row. Change tension to 7 and knit 10 more rows. Pick up first row of waistband and cast off. Remove waste yarn.
  Repeat for second leg.

Cuffs: Place 2 stitches of cast on row of leg onto every one of 60 needles. With tension at 6, to ensure a tight rib, knit 15 rows in blue. Drop every third stitch. Pick up stitches with latchet tool to form rib and cast off.
  Repeat for second cuff.

Braces: Using double-bed machine or ribber attachment and tension at 5, cast on 7 needles on front bed and 8 needles on back bed. Knit 2 rows. Transfer every third needle for buttonholes. Knit 148 more rows. Transfer every third needle for buttonholes. Knit 2 rows. Cast off.

To finish: Pin and steam press. When pinning together make sure that you match the crotch seams on each leg. Sew together, starting with the leg seams. Thread waistband with elastic, attach buttons and braces and complete sewing up.

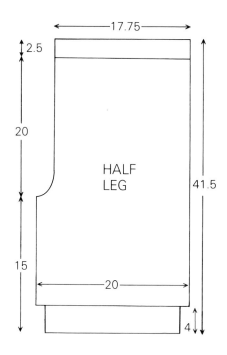

HALF LEG

17.75

2.5

20

41.5

20

15

4

4 The Sophisticated Baby

The sophisticated baby is self-possessed and has no need to draw attention to himself. This baby has natural 'presence' at an early age. Unlike his peers, the sophisticated baby watches rather than participates, is still rather than active, and makes the perfect model for clothes that other babies would either ruin immediately or look most ill at ease in. Because of his personality and poise this baby can wear dark colours; and a sophisticated baby girl looks good in formal dresses. To reflect the sophistication of this baby, his or her clothes are simple, almost austere, and the colours mostly dark.

Yet no baby, however sophisticated, is completely lacking in playfulness, so to start with there's a romper suit in bold stripes of burgundy, dark green, blue and beige. The second garment is a loose, dark, birdseye, Fair Isle patterned cardigan in dark green and navy, with striped ribs that match the romper suit. To co-ordinate with the cardigan are a pair of matching leggings with striped ribs. To wear under the cardigan I've included a choice of knitted tops. The first is a simple, long-sleeved beige jersey in mercerised cotton with a cabled front, and the second is a short-sleeved shirt in blue mercerised cotton. To complete the sophisticated baby's wardrobe there is a gathered mercerised cotton dress in navy with puff sleeves and dark stripes around the hem.

STRIPED ROMPER SUIT WITH SHORT SLEEVES AND RIBBED SHIRT COLLAR

Adapted from crew neck block, page 13.

Materials
Knitted in Brockwell Wools 4 ply mercerised cotton: 75gms green, 50gms beige, 50gms red, 75gms blue. 7 pearl buttons.

Size
To fit baby aged 9–12 months (80cm).

Tension
Dial number 6
3.1 stitches = 1cm
4.3 rows = 1cm

Machines
Any domestic single-bed machine.

Back: Cast on 25 stitches (8cm) in green. With tension at 6, knit 5 rows. Knit 1 row with tension at 7 and 5 more rows with tension at 6, making sure that on rows 3 and 9 you transfer every sixth stitch to make 3 buttonholes. Pick up cast on edge to make hem.

On rows 11 to 15 cast on 5 stitches (carriage side) every row. Change colour on row 16 and knit in stripes of beige 2 rows, red 2 rows, blue 4 rows, beige 2 rows, red 2 rows, green 4 rows. Cast on 5 stitches (carriage side) on row 16.

On rows 17 and 18 cast on 6 stitches (carriage side), on rows 19, 20, 21, 22, 23 and 24 cast on 5 stitches carriage side. You should now have 97 stitches.

Knit 64 rows in stripes. By row 89 work measures about 19cm. On row 90 decrease 1 stitch both sides and then 1 stitch both sides every eighth row until row

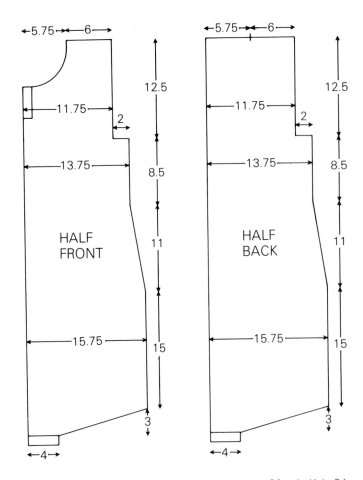

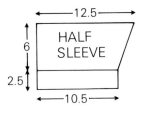

138 (85 stitches and work measures 30cm). Knit 36 rows in stripes until armhole shaping at row 174. On rows 174 and 175 cast off 6 stitches carriage side, leaving 73 stitches. Knit 54 rows until row 229. Cast off 19 stitches both sides for shoulders. Using remaining 35 stitches knit 20 rows for the back collar rib. Drop every third stitch and form rib with latchet tool. Cast off.

Front: Repeat as for back, without buttonholes, until row 196 to start neck band. Put all needles left of centre on hold except 2 central needles. Cast off 3 stitches right of centre and 2 stitches left of centre to make room for ribbed buttonhole band (see diagram 45). From row 197 knit 14 rows keeping stripes; begin neck shaping on row 211 by holding 6 stitches on the neck side. On row 213 hold 1 stitch and hold 2 stitches on rows 215, 217, 219 and 221. Knit 8 rows. On row 229 cast off the remaining 19 stitches on the shoulder side. Push the held stitches into knitting position and knit 20 rows. Form rib as for back. Cast off.

Repeat from row 197 for left side.

Sleeves: From armhole to shoulder seam hook 39 stitches both sides of centre onto needlebed with the wrong side of knitting facing you (78 stitches). Knit 2 rows in blue and decrease 1 stitch both sides. Knit 2 rows in red, 2 rows in beige and decrease 1 stitch both sides. Knit 4 rows in green. Decrease 1 stitch both sides and knit 2 rows in red and 2 rows in beige. Decrease 1 stitch both sides and knit 4 rows in blue. Decrease 1 stitch both sides and knit 2 rows in red, 2 rows in beige. Decrease 1 stitch both sides and knit 4 rows in green. Knit 10 more rows in green and drop every third stitch. Form rib with latchet tool. Cast off.

Repeat for second sleeve.

Front buttonhole band: Pick up 15 stitches down left front opening. Knit 4 rows, transfer third and eighth stitches to make buttonholes and knit 4 more rows. Drop every third stitch and form rib with latchet tool. Cast off.

Repeat for other side band, without buttonholes.

Leg hems: Pick up 39 stitches along leg edges both sides of the side seams and hook along needlebed both sides of centre (see diagram 46). Knit 3 rows in green on tension 6. Transfer 1 stitch 3 needles in from the edge on the buttonhole side and knit 2 rows. Knit 1 row at tension 7 and 2 rows at tension 6. Transfer 1 stitch 3 needles in from the edge on the buttonhole side and knit 3 rows. Pick up cast on row and cast off.

Repeat for second leg.

To finish: Pin and steam press. Sew up seams, matching stripes, and attach buttons to crotch seam and neck band.

diagram 45 Casting off central
needles to make room for buttonhole
placket and sloping neck

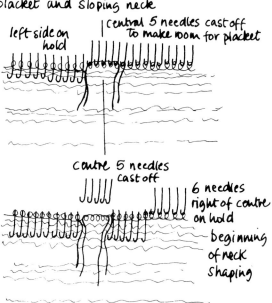

left side on
hold

central 5 needles cast off
to make room for placket

centre 5 needles
cast off

6 needles
right of centre
on hold

beginning
of neck
shaping

diagram 46
cast on for leg hem
with buttonhole at
crotch

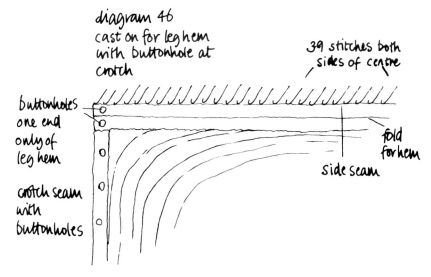

39 stitches both
sides of centre

buttonholes
one end
only of
leg hem

crotch seam
with
buttonholes

fold
for hem

side seam

BIRDSEYE FAIR ISLE
PATTERNED CARDIGAN

Adapted from crew neck block, page 17.

Size
To fit baby aged 12–18 months (80–90cm).

Tension
Dial number 7
3 stitches = 1cm
3.5 rows = 1cm
Patterned punchcard in birdseye Fair Isle pattern (see diagram 47). Punch card before starting to knit.

Machines
Any domestic single-bed machine with a punchcard facility.

Materials
Knitted in Lister Motoravia 4 ply navy wool and Brockwell Wools 4 ply mercerised cotton in green, red and blue. 150gms navy, 60gms green, 25gms red, 25gms blue. 9 dark pearl buttons.

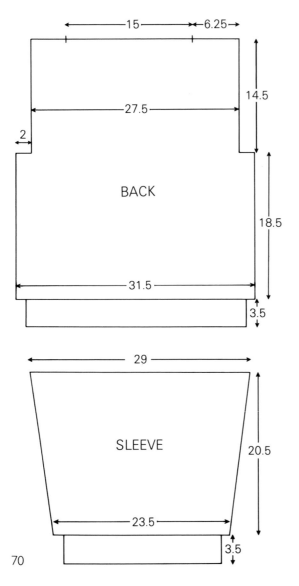

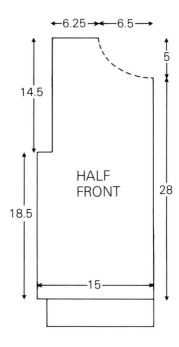

Back: Cast on 94 stitches (31.5cm) in navy. With tension at 6, knit 2 rows navy and 1 row each in red, navy, blue, navy, green and navy. Knit 2 rows in red and 1 row each in blue, navy, green and navy (14 rows total). Drop alternate stitches and form rib with latchet

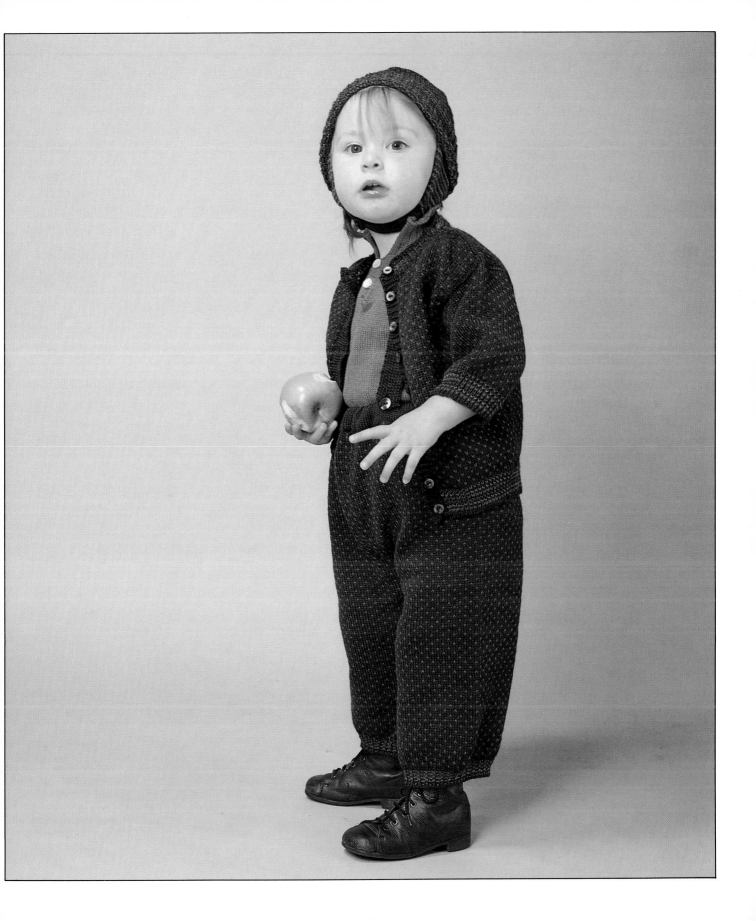

diagram 47

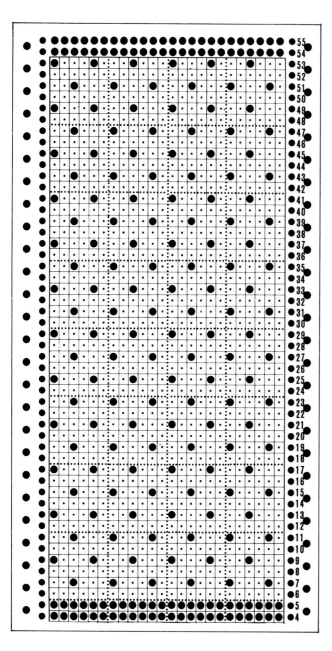

tool. Change to tension 7 and knit 1 row in navy. On next row (row 16) start punchcard pattern on any row number with green in the second yarn feeder and knit in pattern. Start armhole shaping on row 78 by casting off 6 stitches carriage side and cast off another 6 on row 79.

Continue knitting until row 128 (work measures 36.5cm). Cast off 19 stitches both sides for shoulders. Change to tension 6 and knit rib: knit 2 rows in navy and 1 row each in green, navy, red, navy, blue, navy and green. Drop alternate stitches and form rib with latchet tool. Cast off in navy.

Right front: Cast on 45 stitches (15cm) in navy. With tension at 6 knit rib as for back. Pick up rib on row 14. Change to tension 7 and knit 1 row in navy. On row 16 start punchcard with green in second yarn feeder. Knit in pattern. On row 78 start armhole shaping by casting off 6 stitches. Continue knitting until row 110 for neck shaping and hold 4 stitches on centre side. Hold 3 stitches on rows 112 and 114. Hold 2 stitches on rows 116, 118, 120, and 122. Hold 1 stitch on rows 124 and 126. On row 128 cast off remaining 19 stitches for shoulder. Knit neck rib on held stitches as for back.

Repeat for left front, reversing armhole and neck shapings.

Sleeves: Cast on 70 stitches (23.5cm) in navy. With tension at 6, knit rib in stripes as for back. Change to tension 7 and knit 1 row in navy. On row 16 start punchcard pattern with green in second yarn feeder. Knit in pattern. Increase 1 stitch both sides every sixth row until row 70 (88 stitches). Knit 1 row in navy and cast off.

Repeat for second sleeve.

Front buttonhole band: Pick up onto needlebed 88 stitches from right front. With tension at 6, knit 4 rows in navy. Make buttonholes: transfer 1 stitch 3 stitches from top of neck and then every tenth stitch (makes 9 buttonholes). Knit 4 more rows. Drop alternate stitches and form rib with latchet tool. Cast off.

Repeat for left front band without the buttonholes.

To finish: Pin and steam press. Zig-zag edges of knitting with navy cotton on a sewing machine (see diagram 48). Thread through all loose ends and snip off. Sew seams together 1 stitch in from the edge so that the zig-zag does not show. Sew dark pearl buttons onto button band.

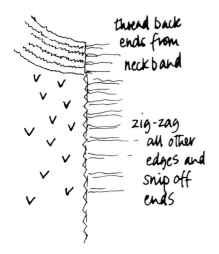

diagram 48

thread back ends from neckband

zig-zag — all other edges and snip off ends

BIRDSEYE FAIR ISLE
PATTERNED LEGGINGS

Adapted from the leggings block, page 28.

Materials
Knitted in Lister Motoravia 4 ply wool in navy and Brockwell Wools 4 ply mercerised cotton in green, red and blue. 170gms navy, 75gms green, 25gms red, 25gms blue. 4 dark pearl buttons. 54cm of 1cm elastic.

Size
To fit baby aged 12–18 months (80–90cm).

Tension
Dial number 7. Ribs tension 5.
3 stitches = 1cm
3.5 rows = 1cm
Pattern punchcard in birdseye Fair Isle pattern (see diagram 47). Punch card before starting to knit.

Machines
Any domestic single-bed machine with a punchcard facility. For the braces, a double-bed machine or a single-bed ribber attachment.

Legs: Cast on 114 stitches (38cm) in navy. With tension at 7, knit 11 rows. Change to tension 8 and knit 1 row. Knit 11 more rows at tension 7. Pick up cast on row of waistband.

Start punchcard pattern (on row 24) with green in second yarn feeder. Knit in pattern. From row 91 to row 101 increase 1 stitch both sides every alternate row until at row 101 there are 126 stitches. Continue knitting until row 178. Knit several rows of waste yarn. Remove knitting from machine.

Leg rib: Place 2 stitches onto each needle from the last row of patterned knitting (63 stitches). Change to tension 6 and return row counter to 178. Knit 1 row each in navy, green, navy, red, navy, blue, navy, green and navy (to row 187). Drop alternate stitches and form rib with latchet tool. Cast off in navy.

Repeat for second leg.

73

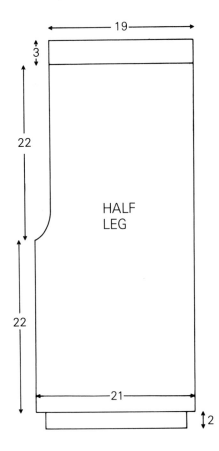

Diagram labels:
- 19
- 3
- 22
- HALF LEG
- 22
- 21
- 2

Braces: Using a double-bed machine or a ribber attachment, tension at 5 (2.5 stitches = 1cm, 3.7 rows = 1cm). Cast on 7 stitches front bed and 8 stitches back bed, in navy. Knit 2 rows. Transfer third stitch on front and back bed to form buttonhole. Continue knitting to row 158. Transfer third stitch for button-hole. Knit 2 rows. Cast off. Sew in yarn at both ends of braces.

To finish: Pin and steam press. Zig-zag edges on sewing machine (see diagram 48) and snip off. Sew leg seams together and then front and back seams. Thread waistband with elastic and sew up waistband. Attach 4 dark pearl buttons front and back for braces.

LONG-SLEEVED CABLED JERSEY

Adapted from the crew neck block, page 13.

Materials
Knitted in Brockwell Wools 4 ply mercerised cotton, in beige: 175gms. 3 pearl buttons.

Size
To fit baby aged 9–12 months (80cm).

Tension
Dial number 6
3.3 stitches = 1cm
4.5 rows = 1cm

Machines
Any domestic single-bed machine.

Back: Cast on 90 stitches (27.5cm). Knit 9 rows at tension 5 for rib. Drop every third stitch and form rib with latchet tool. Change tension to 6 and row counter to 0 and knit until row 90 (20cm). Cast off 7 stitches on carriage side on rows 90 and 91. Knit until row 146 and cast off 18 stitches both sides for shoulders. Change to tension 5 for neck rib and knit 15 rows. Drop every third stitch and form rib with latchet tool. Cast off.

Front: Repeat as for back until row 17. From row 17 cable over 4 central needles every eighth row. Make last cable on row .129. Shape neck on row 133 by pushing all needles left of centre into hold position. Knit the right side and hold 4 stitches on rows 133 and 135, hold 2 stitches on rows 137, 139, 141, 143, 145 and 146. Cast off remaining 18 stitches for shoulder. Push right-side held needles to knit position and repeat neck shaping from row 133 to row 146. Don't cast off shoulder stitches but change to tension 5 and knit 3 rows. Drop every third stitch and form rib with latchet tool. Transfer the third, eighth and thirteenth stitches to form buttonholes. Knit 3 rows, drop every third stitch and form rib with latchet tool. Cast off.

Knit 15 rows on neck needles (40 stitches). Drop every third stitch and form rib with latchet tool. Cast off.

Sleeves: Join shoulder seams. Hook 41 stitches from front and back armhole both sides of centre onto needlebed with wrong side of knitting facing (82

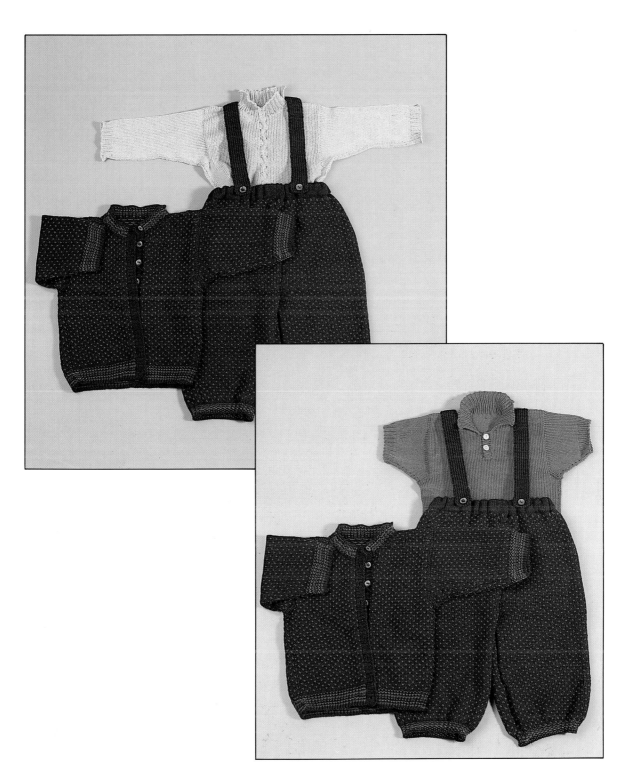

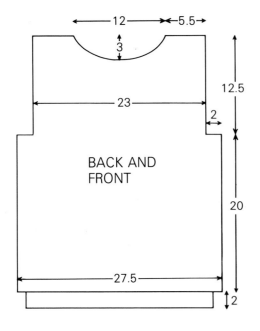

Materials
Knitted in Brockwell Wools 4 ply mercerised cotton in blue: 150gms. 2 pearl buttons. See photo, page 75.

Size
To fit baby aged 9–12 months (80cm).

Tension
Dial number 6
3.3 stitches = 1cm
4.5 rows = 1cm

Machines
Any domestic single-bed machine.

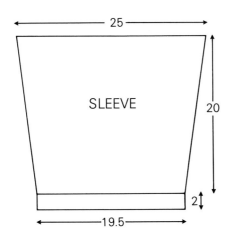

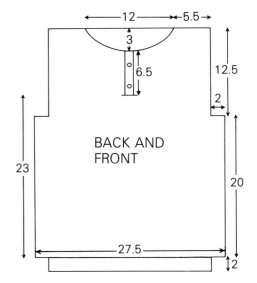

stitches). With tension at 6, knit 10 rows. Decrease 1 stitch both sides. Knit and repeat decrease every 10 rows until 64 stitches remain on needlebed (row 90). Change to tension 5 and knit 9 rows for rib. Drop every third stitch and form rib with latchet tool. Cast off.

Repeat for second sleeve.

To finish: Pin and steam press. Sew seams. Sew three pearl buttons onto left shoulder seam.

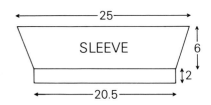

Back: Cast on 90 stitches (27.5cm). Knit 9 rows at tension 5 for the rib. Drop every third stitch and form rib with latchet tool. Change tension to 6 and row counter to 0, and knit until row 90 (20cm). Cast off 7 stitches carriage side on rows 90 and 91. Knit until on row 146 cast off 18 stitches both sides for shoulders. Change to tension 5 and knit 20 rows on remaining 40 neck stitches. Drop every third stitch and form rib with latchet tool. Cast off.

Front: Repeat as for back until row 104 (23cm, excluding rib). Put all needles left of centre on hold except the 2 central needles. Cast off 2 stitches right of centre and 2 stitches left of centre to make room for ribbed buttonhole placket. Continue knitting on right side needles until neck shaping at row 133. Hold 4 stitches neck side on row 133, hold 3 stitches on row 135 and 2 stitches on rows 137, 139, 141, 143 and 145. Hold 1 stitch on row 146. Cast off remaining 18 stitches for shoulder. Change to tension 5 and on right-side held needles knit 20 rows. Drop every third stitch and form rib with latchet tool. Cast off.

Repeat for left side needles from row 105.

Front buttonhole band: Pick up 16 stitches onto needlebed down left front opening. Knit 3 rows at tension 5. Transfer the second and eighth stitches down from neck to make 2 buttonholes. Knit 3 rows, drop every third stitch and form rib with latchet tool. Cast off.

Repeat for right side, without buttonholes.

Sleeves: Join shoulder seams. From armhole to shoulder seam hook 41 stitches both sides of centre onto needlebed, wrong side of knitting facing (82 stitches). With tension at 6, knit 4 rows. Decrease 1 stitch both sides. Knit until row 28, decreasing 1 stitch both sides every 4 rows (68 stitches left). Change to tension 5 and knit 9 rows. Drop every third stitch and form rib with latchet tool. Cast off.

Repeat for second sleeve.

To finish: Pin and steam press. Sew seams and attach 2 pearl buttons onto buttonhole band.

SHORT-SLEEVED GATHERED DRESS

Materials
Knitted in Brockwell Wools 4 ply mercerised cotton: 300gms navy, 25gms red, 25gms green, 25gms beige. 30cm thread elastic for puff sleeves. 3 dark pearl buttons.

Size
To fit baby aged 12–18 months (80–90cm).

Tension
Dial number 6
3.1 stitches = 1cm
4.5 rows = 1cm

Machines
Any domestic single-bed machine.

Back: Cast on 186 stitches (60cm) in navy. Knit 4 rows at tension 6. Change to tension 7 and knit 1 row, then knit 4 rows at tension 6. Pick up cast on row to form hem. Return row counter to 0. Knit in stripes with 1 row each of red, navy, green, navy, red, navy and green. From row 7 continue knitting in navy and start armhole shaping at row 171 (work measures 38cm, excluding hem). On rows 172, 173, 174 and 175 cast off 2 stitches at carriage side on each row. On rows 177, 179, 181, 183 and 185 decrease 1 stitch both sides. Knit several rows of waste yarn. Remove knitting from machine.

With wrong side of knitting facing you put pairs of stitches onto 84 needles (42 both sides of centre). With row counter at 186 and with tension at 6 put all needles left of centre on hold. Knit 1 row each in navy (row 186), beige, navy, green, navy and red. Then from row 192 knit in navy. On row 232 hold 19 stitches right of centre for neck, knit 2 rows and cast off remaining 23 stitches for shoulder. Knit 19 held neck stitches onto waste yarn.

For left side needles, cast on 3 stitches right of centre and repeat from row 186 as for right side. On row 234 cast off extra 3 stitches right of centre. Knit remaining neck stitches onto waste yarn. Remove from machine.

Front: Repeat as for back until row 186 (navy). Knit 1 row each in beige, navy, green, navy and red. Then knit

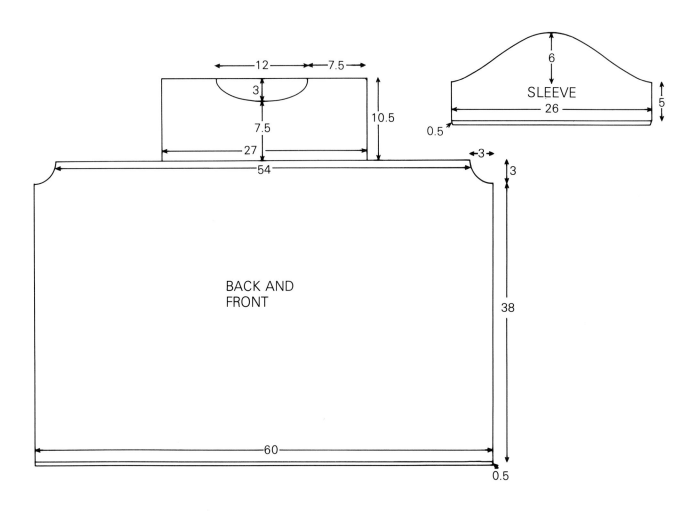

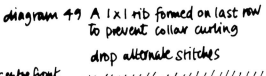

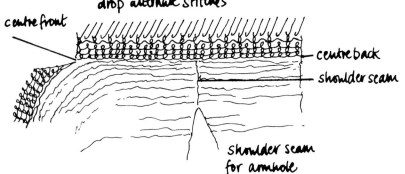

diagram 49 A 1x1 rib formed on last row to prevent collar curling

drop alternate stitches

centre front

centre back

shoulder seam

shoulder seam for armhole

from row 192 in navy. Start neck shaping on row 220. Put all needles left of centre on hold, plus 7 stitches from right of centre. On rows 222 and 224 hold 4 more stitches, on row 226 hold 2 stitches and on rows 228 and 230 hold 1 stitch (19 stitches right of centre on hold). On row 234 cast off 23 stitches for shoulder. Knit several rows of waste yarn on remaining 19 stitches.

Repeat from row 220 for needles left of centre.

Collar: With right side of knitting facing you, pick up stitches from back half and front half neck edges from waste yarn (38 stitches). With tension at 6, knit 10 rows in beige. Drop alternate stitches for 1 row only on the last row and pick up with latchet tool to form rib on this one row. This will stop the collar from curling up (see diagram 49). Cast off.

Repeat for other half of collar.

78

Sleeves: Cast on 80 stitches (26cm) in navy. With tension at 5, knit 4 rows. Change to tension 6 and knit 1 row, then knit 4 more rows at tension 5. Pick up first row to form hem. Change to tension 6 and return row counter to 0. Knit 1 row each in navy, beige, navy, green, navy and red. Then from row 6 knit in navy. From row 23 cast off 3 stitches carriage side each row until row 32. On rows 33 to 36 cast off 2 stitches carriage side. On rows 37 to 40 cast off 1 stitch carriage side. On rows 41 to 48 cast off 3 stitches carriage side. On row 49 cast off remaining 14 stitches.

Repeat for second sleeve.

To finish: Pin and steam press. Sew seams (see diagram 50). If puffed sleeves are required thread fine elastic through the hem of the sleeve. Make 3 button loops on one side of back opening and attach 3 dark pearl buttons to the other side.

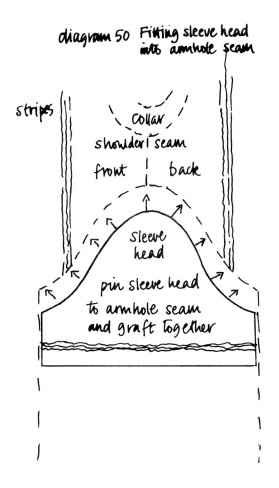

diagram 50 Fitting sleeve head into armhole seam

stripes

collar

shoulder seam

front | back

sleeve head

pin sleeve head to armhole seam and graft together

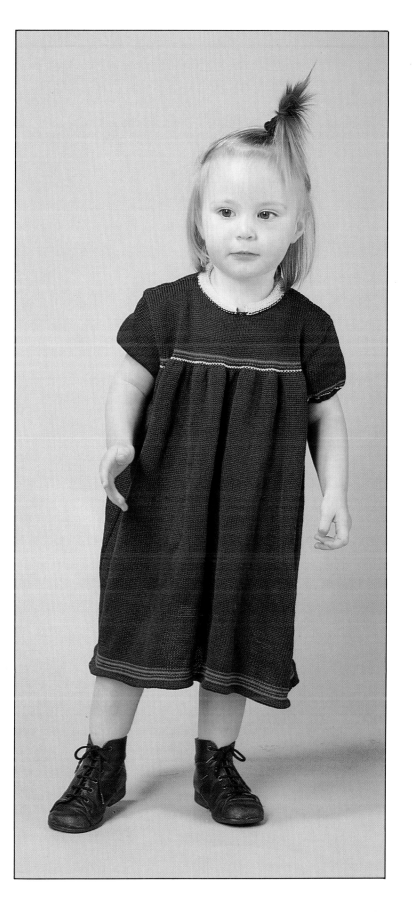

5 The Tweedy Baby

The tweedy baby is seasonal: a winter baby. Dressed entirely in wool, with one garment layered over another to ensure maximum warmth, the tweedy baby is protected against the extremes of winter weather. If the tweedy baby lives in the country where mud and general country conditions prevail, his clothes could become grubby very quickly. However, the very tweediness of his outfits makes him appear much cleaner than he actually is. He is, in all likelihood, slightly predisposed to grubbiness anyway, so the less his clothes show the dirt the better!

The first garment for this baby is a short cross-over Fair Isle waistcoat, ideal as a kidney warmer. This can be worn over anything: a jersey, a dress or a shirt.

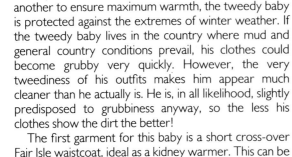

The second garment is a raglan-sleeved, cabled polo neck with striped collar, cuffs and rib. This jersey is long and has a high neck for extra warmth. For even more warmth, the waistcoat can be worn over it providing an extra layer and an effective insulation against the most biting of winter winds.

The practical draught-proof leggings with ribbed cuffs can be worn with the Fair Isle waistcoat and the polo neck jersey and together they make a perfect winter outfit.

The leggings can also be worn with a crew-neck Fair Isle jersey with back opening or a V-neck Fair Isle sleeveless pullover. Both are knitted in warm winter colours.

And for the tweedy baby girl there is a long-sleeved Fair Isle wool frock with striped collar and cuffs. For extra cosiness the frock can be worn with both the leggings and the waistcoat.

No baby dressed in these outfits should feel cold, even on the most wintery of days.

CROSS-OVER
FAIR ISLE WAISTCOAT

Materials
Knitted in Lister Motoravia 4 ply wool: 50gms dark stone, 15gms turquoise, 25gms Arctic white, 25gms navy. Rowan Yarns 4 ply wool: 25gms mauve. 2 pearl buttons.

Size
To fit baby aged up to 9 months (80cm).

Tension
Dial number 6
3.1 stitches = 1cm
3.6 rows = 1cm
Pattern punchcard in Fair Isle pattern (see diagram 51).
Punch card before starting to knit.

Machines
Any domestic single-bed machine with a punchcard facility.

Back: Cast on 80 stitches (26cm) in dark stone. With tension at 6, knit 6 rows. Change tension to 7 and knit 1 row. Then knit 6 rows at tension 6. Pick up cast on row. Return row counter to 0. Knit 2 rows. Thread turquoise through second yarn feeder and start punchcard at row number 1 on row 3. Knit 10 rows in pattern and on row 13 cast off 9 stitches both sides for armholes. Change second feeder yarn to mauve, knit 10 rows, change second feeder to white and knit 1 row. Change second feeder to navy, knit 10 rows, change second feeder to turquoise, knit 10 rows, change second feeder to white and knit 1 row. Change second feeder to mauve, knit 10 rows, change second feeder to navy, knit 10 rows, change second feeder to white and knit 1 row. Change second feeder to turquoise, knit 10 rows,

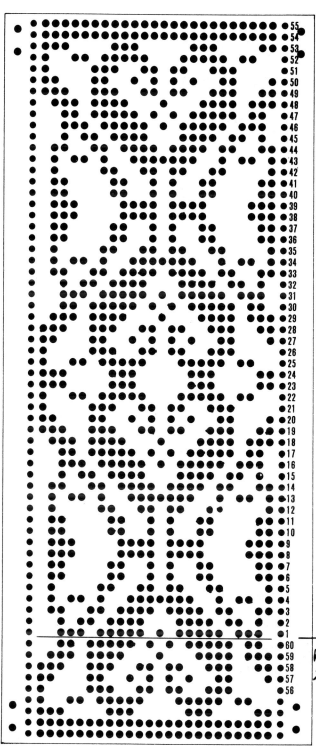

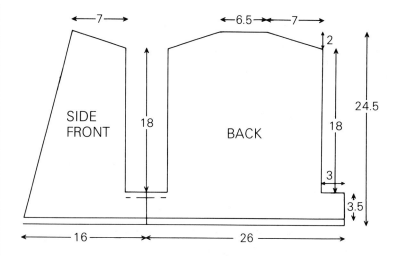

change second feeder to mauve and knit 2 rows. On row 66 hold 7 stitches non-carriage side for one shoulder. Repeat holding 7 stitches for each shoulder on rows 67, 68, 69, 70 and 71 until 21 stitches held for both shoulders. Knit one row and cast off shoulders on row 72. On remaining 20 neck stitches knit 5 rows in dark stone at tension 6, knit one row at tension 7 and 5 rows at tension 6. Pick up first row of neck hem and cast off.

Side front: Cast on 49 stitches (16cm) in dark stone. With tension at 6, knit 6 rows. Change tension to 7 and knit 1 row. Then knit 6 rows at tension 6. Pick up cast on row for hem. Return row counter to 0. Knit 2 rows. Thread turquoise through second yarn feeder and start punchcard at row number 1 on row 3. Knit 10 rows, cast off 9 stitches one side for armhole and decrease 1 stitch on the other side. Continue patterning as for back. Continue to decrease 1 stitch every third row until a further 18 stitches have been decreased over 59

start punchcard here, change colour in 2nd feeder as in pattern

diagram 51

rows (row 72). For last mauve section from row 66 hold 7 stitches on the shoulder side. Repeat on rows 68 and 70 until there are 21 stitches held for the shoulder. Knit 2 rows and cast off on row 72.

Repeat, reversing shapings for second half of front. Make two buttonholes on row 26. Make the first buttonhole 4 stitches in from the front edge and make the second 10 stitches in from the front edge.

Armhole edgings: Sew shoulder seams together. From shoulder seam place 55 stitches from the front and back armholes both sides of centre (110 stitches). In dark stone and at tension 6 knit 5 rows decreasing 1 stitch both sides every row. Knit 1 row at tension 7 and then knit 5 rows at tension 6 increasing 1 stitch both sides every row. Pick up first row and cast off.

Repeat for second armhole edging.

Front edging: From centre back to hem folds pick up onto needlebed 80 stitches both sides of centre (160 stitches). Knit 5 rows at tension 6, 1 row at tension 7 and 5 more rows at tension 6. Pick up first row and cast off.

To finish: Pin and steam press. Sew edgings and side seams together. Attach two pearl buttons opposite the buttonholes.

Machines
Any domestic single-bed machine.

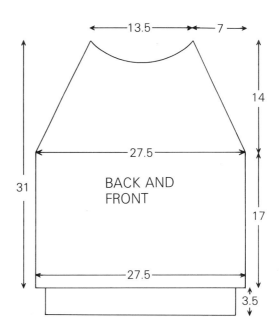

RAGLAN-SLEEVED, CABLED POLO NECK WITH STRIPED COLLAR, CUFFS AND RIB

Adapted from raglan-sleeve block with wide high neck, page 24.

Materials
Knitted in Lister Richmond double knitting wool: 125gms domino; and Lister Motoravia double knitting wool: 25gms pink, 25gms blue, 25gms turquoise.

Size
To fit baby aged 9–12 months (80cm).

Tension
Dial number 4
1.75 stitches = 1cm
2.75 rows = 1cm

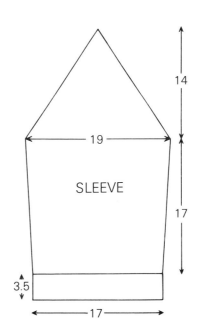

Front: Knit as for back until row 77 and then begin neck shaping. Hold all stitches left of centre and 5 right of centre. Hold 1 stitch every row and continue to decrease for raglan sleeve on the right side. On row 84, with all stitches on hold on the right side, push into action all needles left of centre except the 5 needles closest to centre. Change row counter to 77 and with carriage on the left shape left side and decrease for raglan sleeve as for right side until row 84.

Repeat neck rib as for back.

Sleeves: Cast on 15 alternate stitches over 30 needles. Leave those needles not cast on out of action. With tension at 7, knit in stripes as for back. Form rib with latchet hook as for back. Change tension to 4 and row counter to 0. Form 4 cables over 4 stitches on last row of rib, leaving 1 stitch before side cables and 3 stitches in between the others. On rows 20 and 40 increase 1 stitch both sides (34 stitches). On row 46 begin decreasing for raglan. Decrease 1 stitch both sides on rows 46, 50, 54 and 58 and thereafter every 2 rows over the next 26 rows until by row 84 no stitches remain.

Repeat for second sleeve.

To finish: Steam press. Pin and sew seams.

Back: Cast on 24 alternate stitches over 48 needles in domino. Leave those needles not cast on out of action. With tension at 7, knit 2 rows in domino, 1 row in blue, 2 rows in domino, 1 row in turquoise, 2 rows in domino and 1 row in pink. Repeat stripes until row 15. Pick up alternate stitches with latchet hook to make rib. Change tension dial to 4 and row counter to 0. Make cables over 4 stitches in the last row of rib, then every sixth row, leaving 3 stitches between cables (7 cables). On row 46 begin decreasing for raglan sleeve. Decrease 1 stitch both sides on rows 46, 47, 48 and 49 and then every 4 rows until row 84 (24 stitches left for neck).

For the neck rib, change tension to 7. On the remaining 24 stitches remove alternate stitches and place on waste yarn. Knit 1 row in turquoise, 2 rows in domino, 1 row in pink, 2 rows in domino, 1 row in blue and 2 rows in domino. Repeat stripe sequence. Knit 2 more rows in domino and 1 row in turquoise (21 rows rib). Pick up alternate stitches from waste yarn with latchet hook to form rib. Cast off in domino.

84

LEGGINGS WITH RIBBED CUFFS

Adapted from leggings block, page 28

Materials
Knitted in Lister Motoravia 4 ply wool: 175gms black. 52cm of 2cm elastic. See photo, page 86.

Size
To fit baby aged 12–18 months (90cm).

Tension
Dial number 7
3 stitches = 1cm
4 rows = 1cm

Machines
Any domestic single-bed machine.

Legs: Cast on 138 stitches. Knit 84 rows. Over next 7 rows decrease 1 stitch both sides. Knit until row 180.

Add a fine contrasting yarn for 1 row (so you can see the row to pick up for the waistband) and knit 10 rows. Change tension to 9 for 1 row for waistband fold and knit 10 more rows at tension 7. Pick up marked row. Cast off. Remove contrasting yarn.

Repeat for second leg.

Cuffs: Place 2 stitches from cast on row onto every one of 69 needles. With tension at 6, knit 36 rows. Drop alternate pairs of stitches. Pick up stitches with latchet hook to form rib. Cast off.

Repeat for second cuff.

To finish: Pin flat and steam press. Make sure when pinning together that the crotch seams are matched on each leg. Sew leg seams first, then other seams. Thread waistband with elastic and sew up waistband.

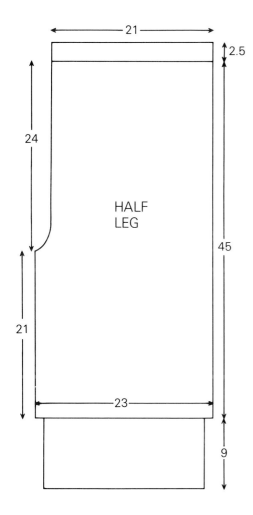

CREW NECK FAIR ISLE JERSEY WITH BACK OPENING

Materials
Knitted in Lister Motoravia 4 ply wool: 125gms school grey, 25gms black. Rowan Yarns fine nepp 3 ply wool: 25gms yellow, 25gms rust, 25gms purple. Lister Richmond double knitting wool: 50gms dice. 4 black buttons.

Size
To fit baby aged 12–18 months (90cm).

Tension
Dial number 7
3 stitches = 1cm
3.7 rows = 1cm
Pattern punchcard in Fair Isle pattern (see diagram 52, page 89). Punch card before starting to knit.

Machines
Any domestic single-bed machine with punchcard facility.

Back: Cast on 94 stitches (31.5cm) in grey. With tension at 5, knit 14 rows. Drop every third stitch and then pick up to form rib. Change tension to 7 and row counter to 0. On row 1 start the punchcard on row 1 and change colours as shown in diagram 52. Knit in pattern. On row 80 cast off 6 stitches both sides for armholes. Continue until row 100. Divide for back opening by putting the needles left of centre on hold (41 stitches). Note punchcard row number. Continue knitting on right side needles until row 134. Cast off 19 stitches for shoulder. Change to tension 5, knit 9 rows on remaining 22 stitches in grey. Drop every third stitch and pick up with latchet hook to form rib. Cast off.

Repeat from row 100 for other side, remembering to turn back punchcard.

Front: Cast on 94 stitches in grey. Knit as for back until row 80. Cast off 6 stitches both sides for armholes. Continue until row 116 and note punchcard row number. Divide for neck by putting half of the needles on hold. For the neck shaping hold 4 needles on rows 116 and 118. Hold 2 needles on rows 120, 122, 124, 126, 128, 130 and 132. On row 134 cast off remaining 19 stitches for shoulder.

85

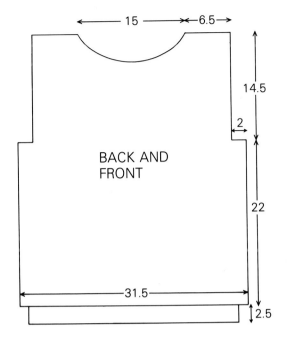

← 15 → ← 6.5 →

BACK AND
FRONT

14.5

2

22

31.5

2.5

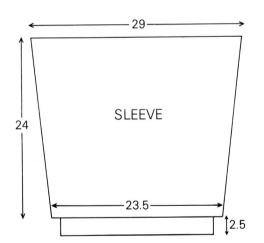

← 29 →

24

SLEEVE

23.5

2.5

Repeat for the other side of neck from row 116 (remembering to turn punchcard back). Cast off second shoulder. Change to tension 5 and on remaining 44 held stitches knit 9 rows in grey. Drop every third stitch. Pick up stitches with latchet hook to form rib. Cast off.

Sleeves: Hook 44 stitches from the armholes of back and front both sides of centre (88 stitches) onto needlebed. Start punchcard at row 1, follow diagram 52 for colour changes and knit 10 rows. Decrease 1 stitch both sides. Repeat decrease every tenth row including row 90 (70 stitches). Change to tension 5 and knit 14 rows in grey. Drop every third stitch. Pick up stitches with latchet hook to form rib. Cast off.

Repeat for second sleeve.

Back neck opening: Pick up 36 stitches one side of opening only. With tension at 5, knit 5 rows. Make 4 buttonholes every 9 stitches. Knit 4 more rows. Drop every third stitch. Pick up stitches with latchet hook to form rib. Cast off.

To finish: Steam press. Sew side seams, then arm and shoulder seams. Attach 4 buttons opposite buttonholes. Sew down bottom end of back neck opening (see diagram 53).

diagram 53

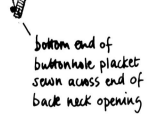

bottom end of
buttonhole placket
sewn across end of
back neck opening

V-NECK FAIR ISLE
SLEEVELESS PULLOVER

Materials
Knitted in Lister Motoravia 4 ply wool: 100gms black. Rowan Yarns fine nepp 3 ply wool: 25gms yellow, 25gms rust, 25gms purple. Rowan Yarns fine cotton chenille 4 ply/double knitting: 25gms saville. Lister Richmond double knitting: 25gms dice. See photo, page 86.

Size
To fit baby aged 12–18 months (90cm).

Tension
Dial number 7
3 stitches = 1cm
3.7 rows = 1cm
Pattern punchcard in Fair Isle pattern (see diagram 54). Punch card before starting to knit.

Machines
Any domestic single-bed machine with a punchcard facility.

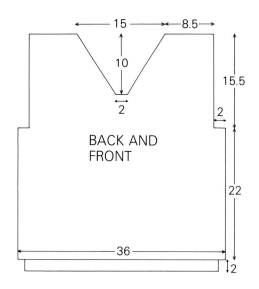

Back: Cast on 108 stitches in black. With tension at 5, knit 12 rows. Drop every third stitch. Pick up stitches with latchet hook to form rib. Change row counter to 0 and tension to 7. On row 1 begin punchcard at row 1. Knit in pattern, changing colours as shown in diagram 54, until row 82. Cast off 6 stitches both sides for armholes. Continue until row 140. Cast off 25 stitches both sides for shoulders. Knit neck rib on remaining 46 stitches in black. Change to tension 5, knit 6 rows. Drop every third stitch. Pick up stitches with latchet hook to form rib. Cast off.

Front: Cast on 108 stitches in black. Knit as for back until row 102. To make neck, cast off central 6 stitches. (Make a note of the punchcard row number.) Push half the needles into hold position (45 stitches). Decrease 1 stitch every row at the neck edge, 4 times. Then decrease 1 stitch at the neck edge every other row, 16 times, until row 138. Knit 2 rows. Cast off remaining 25 stitches for shoulder.

Repeat shaping for second side from row 102, remembering to turn punchcard back. Cast off 25 stitches for second shoulder.

Neck rib: Hook 35 stitches from one side of front V-neck onto the needlebed. With tension at 5, knit 6 rows in black. Drop every third stitch. Pick up with latchet hook to form rib. Cast off.

Repeat for second side.

Armhole rib: Sew shoulder seams together. Pick up 45 stitches from front and back armholes both sides of shoulder seam (90 stitches) onto needlebed. With tension at 5, knit 6 rows in black. Drop every third stitch. Pick up stitches with latchet hook to form rib. Cast off.

Repeat for other armhole.

To finish: Steam press. Sew side seams and front seam at V-neck.

diagram 52

On rows marked ✳ alternate
between rust and purple

diagram 54

		Feeder B

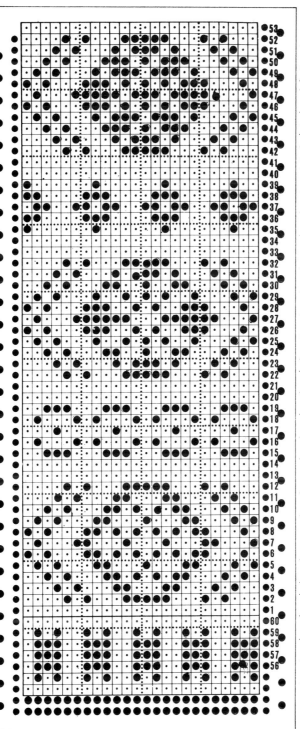

diagram 52			diagram 54	
✳	53		52-53-54	yellow
			50-51	rust
dice	48-49-50-51-52		48-49	purple
			46-47	empty
empty	46-47		44-45	dice
black	44-45		43	rust
yellow	43		41-42	dice
black	41-42		39-40	empty
empty	39-40		37-38	purple
			35-36	rust
dice	34-35-36-37-38			
			32-33-34	yellow
✳	33		30-31	rust
			28-29	purple
dice	28-29-30-31-32		26-27	empty
			24-25	dice
empty	26-27		23	rust
black	24-25		21-22	dice
yellow	23		19-20	empty
black	21-22		17-18	purple
empty	19-20		15-16	rust
			12-13-14	yellow
dice	14-15-16-17-18		10-11	rust
✳	13		8-9	purple
			6-7	empty
dice	8-9-10-11-12		4-5	dice
			3	rust
empty	6-7		1-2	dice
black	4-5		59-60	empty
yellow	3		57-58	purple
black	1-2		55-56	rust
empty	59-60			
dice	54-55-56-57-58			

GATHERED LONG-SLEEVED
FAIR ISLE FROCK

Materials

Knitted in Lister Motoravia 4 ply wool: 200gms black, 40gms turquoise, 25gms crushed mulberry, 40gms misty heather. Lister Richmond double knitting: 25gms dice. Rowan Yarns fine nepp 3 ply: 40gms blue. 4 dark pearl buttons.

Size

To fit baby aged 9–12 months (80cm).

Tension

Dial number 6
3.3 stitches = 1cm
4.2 rows = 1cm
Punchcard pattern in Fair Isle pattern (see diagram 55).
Punch card before starting to knit.

Machines

Any domestic single-bed machine with a punchcard facility.

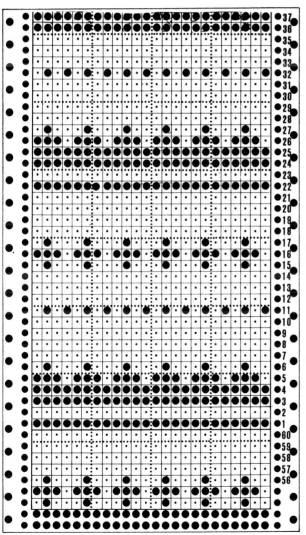

Row	Colour
37	crushed mulberry
33-34-35-36	empty
29-30-31-32	misty heather
28	empty
27	crushed mulberry
23-24-25-26	empty
20-21-22	turquoise
17-18-19	empty
16	white / dice
12-13-14-15	empty
8-9-10-11	blue
7	empty
6	crushed mulberry
2-3-4-5	empty
59-60-1	turquoise
56-57-58	empty

diagram 55

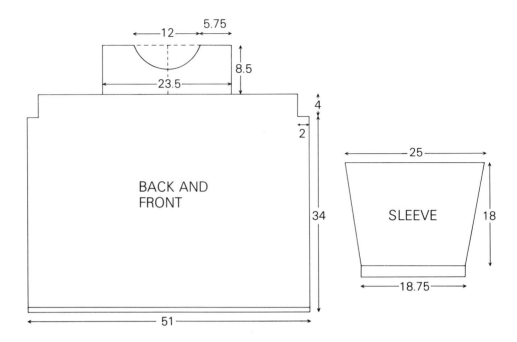

Back: Cast on 168 stitches in black. With tension at 6, knit 4 rows. Knit 1 row at tension 7 and 4 rows at tension 6. Pick up cast on row to make hem. Turn row counter to 0 and on row 1 begin punchcard at row number 60, changing colours as shown in diagram 55. Knit in pattern. At row 143 (34cm) cast off 6 stitches both sides for armholes. Continue until row 159. Note punchcard row number. Knit several rows of waste yarn. Remove knitting. Pick up pairs of stitches onto 78 needles (39 each side of centre). Split knitting for back opening by placing 39 stitches on hold. Continue knitting on remaining needles until row 195. Cast off 19 stitches shoulder side.

To knit neck rib on remaining 20 stitches, knit 2 rows in dice, 1 row in crushed mulberry, 2 rows in dice, 1 row in turquoise, 2 rows in dice and 1 row in blue. Repeat these 9 rows. Then knit 2 rows in dice, 1 row in crushed mulberry, 2 rows in dice, 1 row in turquoise and 2 rows in dice. Drop alternate stitches to make a 1 × 1 rib. Pick up stitches with latchet hook to form rib and cast off in dice.

Repeat from row 160 for second side, remembering to turn punchcard back, and cast on an extra 4 stitches at the centre for the button overlap. Cast these 4 off before starting neck rib.

Front: Repeat as for back (but do not split knitting) in pattern until row 176. Note punchcard row number.

Split knitting for neck shaping by putting left side needles (39) on hold, plus 5 needles from right of centre. Hold 3 stitches neck side on rows 178 and 180. Hold 2 stitches on rows 182 and 184. Hold 1 stitch on rows 186, 188, 190, 192 and 194. Cast off remaining 19 stitches for shoulder on row 195.

Repeat from row 176 for left side neck shaping, remembering to turn punchcard back. On row 196 start neck rib on 40 held stitches. Make rib in stripe sequence as for back. Cast off.

Sleeves: Sew the shoulder seams. Place 41 stitches from front and back armholes both sides of centre onto needlebed (82 stitches). Start punchcard on row number 1. Knit 2 rows, decrease 1 stitch both sides. Change colours as in diagram 55, as before. Decrease 1 stitch both sides every eighth row until row 74 (62 stitches). Knit 2 rows. For rib, knit 2 rows in dice, 1 row in turquoise, 2 rows in dice, 1 row in blue, 2 rows in dice, 1 row in crushed mulberry and 1 row in dice. Drop every alternate stitch to make a 1 × 1 rib. Pick up stitches with latchet tool to form rib. Cast off in dice.

Repeat for second sleeve.

To finish: Either zig-zag edges neatly on sewing machine and cut off ends or sew them in by hand. Steam press and pin together. Sew seams. Crochet 4 buttonhole loops in black wool onto back opening. Sew on 4 dark pearl buttons.

92

6 The Outrageous Baby

The outrageous baby is too young for inhibitions. He or she is a shameless flirt, bestowing a ravishing smile upon every gullible admirer – a perfect seducer. Such babies deserve an outfit that enhances their roles as charismatic charmers. Like them, it must seduce. Either it must be very dark and glittery, or, fantastically bright. Above all it must be immediately noticeable, and suitably outrageous.

The first of these outrageous outfits is ideal for a winter party, for it is sparkling, velvety and dark, with occasional stripes of metallic red. It comprises three garments: bibbed trousers with braces, striped in black chenille, sparkling midnight blue and scarlet rayon, worn over a roll-neck midnight blue long-sleeved jersey. Over these two garments can be worn a round-necked buttoned jacket striped to match the dungarees. This baby is indeed dressed to kill, in a suit which is not just outrageous but in addition, practical and very warm.

The second outfit is equally outrageous though rather more brash: more suited to a baby who charms with irrepressible chuckles rather than beguiling smiles. It is ideal for a summer party when your baby wants to look summery but stay warm. To fulfil these requirements it must be bright – very bright – and a long-sleeved romper suit with turquoise soles and zip front, patterned in neon-bright cottons on a random black and white ground is perfect for an outrageous baby on a summer's day. Over this romper suit, in case the day turns cloudy or wet, can be worn a matching stud-fastening jacket knitted in the same bright neon colours and pattern.

No baby dressed in either of these outrageous outfits could possibly pass unnoticed or fail to arouse enormous admiration.

SPARKLY STRIPED DUNGAREES

Materials
Knitted in Argyll's ziggy cone: 80gms blue, 5gms black. Silverknit rayon: 5gms red. Rowan Yarns chenille: 80gms black. 2 dark pearl buttons.

Size
To fit baby aged 12–18 months (90cm).

Tension
Dial number 9
2.3 stitches = 1cm
3.3 rows = 1cm

Machines
Any domestic single-bed machine.

Legs: Cast on 100 stitches (44cm) in blue. Knit in stripes of 4 rows blue, 4 rows black chenille, 1 row red, 1 row black ziggy cone. Repeat until row 90. On rows 90, 92, 94, 96 and 98 decrease 1 stitch both sides leaving 90 stitches (40cm). Continue striping until row 166 (50cm). Knit several rows in waste yarn and remove knitting from machine.

Repeat for second leg.

Waistband and bib: Using the last row before waste yarn, place each leg both sides of the centre on the needlebed. Hook every third and fourth stitch onto the same needle (starting from the centre of each leg) so that each leg has 68 needles. Return row counter to 0. Knit 7 rows in blue. Push all needles carriage side into hold position except the 48 nearest the edge. Knit 1 row at tension 10, 7 more rows at tension 9, pick up 48 stitches from the first row of the waistband and cast off those 48 stitches.

Remove carriage to the other side. Push back into

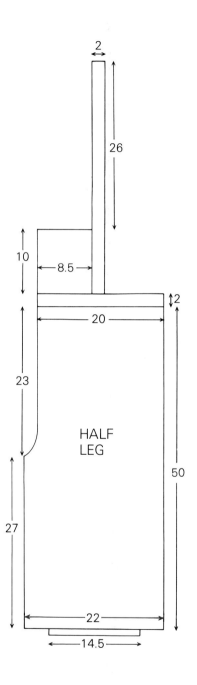

knitting position 48 stitches nearest carriage and repeat from row 7. Cast off second side.

This leaves 40 stitches (17cm) for the bib. Return row counter to 0 and push all needles into knit position. Begin striping with 4 rows of black chenille, I row red, I row black ziggy cone and 4 rows blue. Continue until row 33 (10cm). Knit I row at tension 7 in blue and 2 rows at tension 6. (This tighter tension ensures that the edge does not curl.) Pick up last blue row before yarn changed to chenille on row 30. Cast off.

Trouser hems: Place cast on trouser edge onto 67 needles (29cm), hooking every second and third stitch onto the same needle. At tension 9, knit 4 rows in black chenille, at tension 7 knit I row in blue and at tension 6 knit only 2 rows of blue (to prevent the hem curling). Pick up the first chenille row and cast off.

Braces and bib edge: Hook 20 stitches along the side of the bib onto the needlebed. Put these on hold. Cast on 60 stitches next to the 20 on hold, in blue. Knit 3 rows at tension 9 on the 60 cast on stitches and transfer the fifty-sixth stitch for a buttonhole. Push the 20 held needles into knit position and knit 4 rows across the 80 stitches. Put the 20 back on hold. Knit I row at tension 10 across the 60 needles, 4 rows at tension 9 and transfer the fifty-sixth stitch for a buttonhole. Knit 3 more rows. Pick up the first cast on row from the 60 needles and cast them off. Push the 20 held needles into knit position and knit 3 rows. Knit I row at tension 10 and 7 more rows at tension 9. Pick up the cast on row of bib and cast off.

Repeat for other side of bib.

To finish: Steam press. Pin and sew inside legs edge to edge, matching the stripes across the front and back seams. Secure edge of bib to waistband. Sew the buttons onto the waistband.

SPARKLY SWEATER

Materials
Knitted in Argyll's ziggy cone blue: 125gms.

Size
To fit baby aged 12–18 months (90cm).

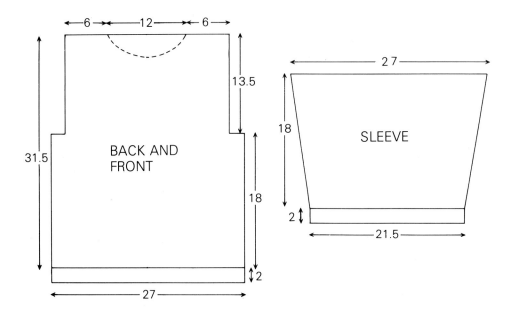

Tension
Dial number 9
2.7 stitches = 1cm
3.5 rows = 1cm

Machines
Any domestic single-bed machine.

Back: Cast on 72 stitches (27cm). Knit 8 rows at tension 8, 1 row at tension 10 and 8 rows at tension 8. Pick up cast on row of hem. Turn row counter to 0 and knit to row 63 (18cm). For armhole shaping, cast off 4 stitches on row 63, carriage side, and 4 stitches on row 64, carriage side. Knit to row 110. Cast off 16 stitches both sides for shoulders. On remaining 32 neck stitches knit 21 rows. Cast off neck on row 131.

Front: Knit as for back until row 96. Divide front for neck shaping. Put half the needles on hold. On row 96 hold 4 needles nearest centre, on rows 98 to 108 hold 2 needles every 2 rows. Knit 2 rows. Cast off shoulder (the unheld 16 stitches) on row 110.

Repeat for second half of neck shaping, after returning row counter to 96. Cast off second shoulder. Knit 21 rows on remaining 32 neck stitches. Cast off neck.

Sleeves: Hook up onto needlebed 36 stitches from each armhole both sides of shoulder seam (total 72 stitches, 27cm). Knit 8 rows and decrease 1 stitch both sides. Repeat decrease on rows 12, 16, 24, 32, 40 and 48 (58 stitches remain). Continue knitting until row 63 (18cm). For hem, knit 8 rows at tension 8, 1 row at tension 10 and 8 more rows at tension 8. Pick up first row of hem. Cast off.

Repeat for second sleeve.

To finish: Pin garment flat and steam press. Pin together and sew seams edge to edge.

ROUND-NECKED SPARKLY JACKET WITH BUTTON FRONT

Materials
Knitted in Argyll's ziggy cone: 70gms blue, and 5gms black. Silverknit red rayon: 5gms. Rowans Yarns black chenille: 70gms. 12 black buttons. See photo, page 96.

Size
To fit baby aged 12–18 months (90cm).

Tension
Dial number 9
2.7 stitches = 1cm
3.5 rows = 1cm

Machines
Any domestic single-bed machine.

Back: Cast on 76 stitches (28cm) in blue. Knit 6 rows at tension 9, 1 row at tension 10 and 6 rows at tension 9. Pick up first row of hem. Return row counter to 0. Knit in stripes of 4 rows black chenille, 1 row red, 1 row ziggy cone black, 4 rows blue. Repeat sequence until row 70 (20cm). For armhole shaping, cast off 4 stitches carriage side. Cast off 4 stitches carriage side on next row. Continue striping sequence until row 119. Cast off 18 stitches carriage side for shoulder. Knit across and cast off 18 stitches for other shoulder (6.5cm each shoulder). Knit 4 rows in blue on central 32 stitches (12cm), 1 row at tension 10 and 4 more rows at tension 9. Pick up first row of neck hem. Cast off.

Right front: Cast on 38 stitches in blue. Repeat as for back until row 70 or 71 (depending on which side carriage is) and cast off 4 stitches for armhole shaping. Continue as for back until row 108 to start of neck shaping. Hold 3 stitches on the opposite side from armhole shaping on rows 108, 110, 112, 114 and 116. Hold 1 stitch on row 118. (If carriage is on the wrong side for neck shaping on these rows, hold on odd number rows instead.) Cast off 18 unheld stitches for shoulder. For the neck edging use the remaining 16 held needles. Knit 4 rows in blue at tension 9, 1 row at tension 10 and 4 more rows at tension 9. Pick up first row of neck edging and cast off.

Repeat, reversing shapings, for second half of front.

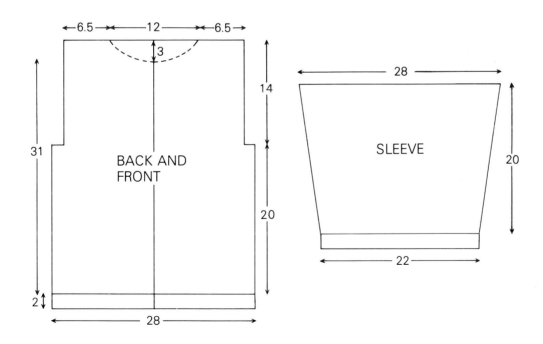

Sleeves: Place front and back armholes onto 38 needles both sides of centre (76 stitches, 28cm). At tension 9, knit in stripes of 4 rows black chenille, 1 row red, 1 row ziggy cone black, 4 rows blue. Beginning on row 10, decrease 2 stitches (1 either side) every 10 rows until row 50 and then on rows 55, 60 and 65 (60 stitches remain). On row 70 start hem in blue. Knit 6 rows at tension 9, 1 row at tension 10 and 6 more rows at tension 9. Pick up first row of hem and cast off.

Repeat for second sleeve.

Front edgings: Place centre front, wrong side facing, onto 87 needles. In blue knit 3 rows and transfer the second and thereafter every seventh stitch to form buttonholes. Knit 3 more rows. Knit 1 row at tension 10 and then 3 more rows, transferring stitches as before for buttonholes. Knit 3 more rows. Pick up first row of edging. Cast off.

Repeat for second front edging without buttonholes.

To finish: Steam press then pin seams. Tie or weave together all loose ends and then sew seams edge to edge making sure that the stripes match across seams. Attach buttons opposite buttonholes.

ROMPER SUIT WITH FRONT ZIP AND CREW NECK

Materials
Knitted in Brockwell Wools 2 ply white and black cotton (knitted together in same feeder) and Brockwell wools 4 ply cotton in emerald green, turquoise, apple green, shocking pink, orange and lemon yellow. Total weight of yarn required, 350gms. A 40cm zip.

Size
To fit baby aged up to 18 months (90cm).

Tension
Dial number 7
3.3 stitches = 1cm
3.3 rows = 1cm
Pattern punchcard in jacquard pattern (see diagram 56). Punch card before starting to knit.

diagram 56

Machines
Any domestic single-bed machine with punchcard facility.

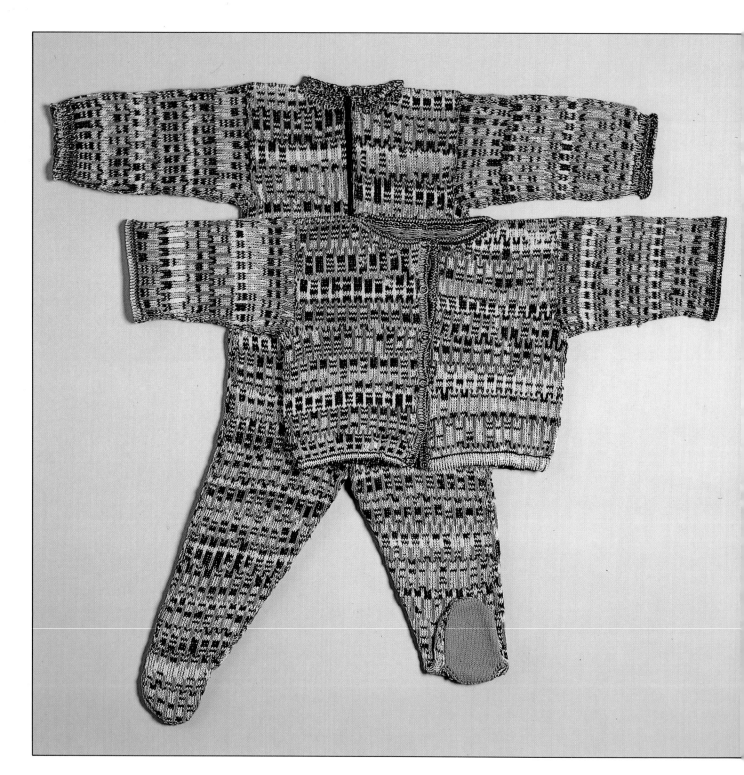

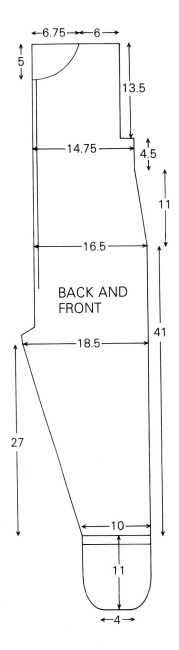

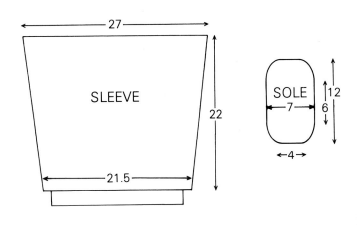

Right back: Cast on 33 stitches (10cm) in black and white together. Knit 2 rows. Prepare to knit in pattern starting punchcard on any number row. Change second colours at random (either on every second, fourth or sixth row) or use the same colour throughout. Increase 1 stitch on left on row 8 and thereafter every third row until row 89 (making 61 stitches, 18.5cm). Knit without increasing until row 98. On row 98 cast off 3 stitches left side and 2 more stitches on the same side on rows 100 and 102. Continue without further decrease until row 142. Decrease 1 stitch on the right side on rows 142, 148, 154, 162, 170 and 178 (48 stitches, 14.75cm). Continue knitting in pattern until row 194.

Cast off 6 stitches right side (42 stitches remain). Continue knitting until row 238. Cast off 20 stitches right side for shoulder. On remaining 22 stitches knit neck rib. At tension 5, knit 8 rows in black and white yarn. Drop alternate stitches and pick up with latchet tool to form rib. Cast off.

Left back: Repeat as for right back, reversing shapings.

Right front: For the foot front, cast on 13 stitches (4cm) in black and white. Knit 2 rows. Prepare to knit in pattern starting punchcard on any row number. Increase 1 stitch both sides on every row until row 12 (33 stitches, 10cm). Knit until row 36. Return row

103

counter to 8 and continue as for right back until row 222 to start of neck shaping (on 42 stitches).

On row 222 hold 6 needles on the right side of knitting. Hold 5 more on row 224, 3 on rows 226, 228 and 230, and 1 on rows 232 and 234. Cast off remaining 20 unheld stitches for shoulder. Knit neck rib on remaining 22 held stitches as for right back. Cast off.

Left front: Repeat as for right front, reversing shapings.

Sleeves: Pick up 88 stitches from the front and back armholes onto the needlebed (44 stitches each armhole either side of shoulder seam). Start punchcard patterning as before. Decrease 1 stitch both sides every eighth row until row 72 (70 stitches, 21.5cm). Knit 10 rows at tension 5, drop alternate stitches and form rib with latchet tool. Cast off.

Soles: Cast on 13 stitches (4cm) in turquoise and knit at tension 7. Increase 1 stitch both sides on every other row until row 10 (23 stitches, 7cm). Knit straight until row 30. Decrease 1 stitch both sides on every other row until row 40 (12cm). Cast off remaining 13 stitches.

To finish: Steam press. Pin sleeve heads into armholes and sew seams. Pin the sides together matching the pattern across the garment and sew, beginning at the wrist and finishing at the ankle. Sew the inside leg seams. Pin and sew the soles to the front feet. Sew in the zip down the front of the suit either by hand or using a zig-zag stitch on a sewing machine. This zig-zag stitch is also very useful for oversewing raw edges before sewing pieces together. Sew back seam.

SHORT PATTERNED JACKET
WITH STUD FASTENING

Materials
Knitted in Brockwell Wools 2 ply white and black cotton (knitted together in the same feeder) and Brockwell Wools 4 ply cotton in emerald green, turquoise, apple green, shocking pink, orange and lemon yellow. Total weight of yarn required, 250gms. 6 press studs. 30cm of 5mm matching tape or elastic. See photo, page 102.

Size
To fit baby aged up to 18 months (90cm).

Tension
Dial number 7
3.3 stitches = 1cm
3.3 rows = 1cm
Pattern punchcard in jacquard pattern (see diagram 56, page 100). Punch card before starting to knit.

Machines
Any domestic single-bed machine with punchcard facility.

Back: Cast on 112 stitches (34cm) in black and white threaded through the same feeder. Knit 4 rows at tension 6, 1 row at tension 7 and 4 rows at tension 6. Pick up cast on row, return row counter to 0 and change tension to 7. Prepare to knit in pattern starting punchcard on any row number. Thread coloured 4 ply cotton through second feeder and change colours randomly (see diagram 56). Knit 53 rows (16cm) in pattern. On row 53 cast off 5 stitches carriage side and on row 54 cast off 5 stitches carriage side. On row 55 cast off 2 stitches carriage side and on row 56 cast off 2 stitches carriage side. Continue knitting until row 99.

Cast off 23 stitches carriage side for shoulder, remove second coloured yarn and change to plain knitting. Knit 1 row in black and white yarn. Cast off 23 stitches for second shoulder. Change tension to 6 and on remaining 52 neck stitches knit 4 rows. Knit 1 row at tension 7 and 4 more rows at tension 6. Pick up the first row of neck hem and cast off.

Right front: Cast on 56 stitches (17cm). Knit as for back until row 53. Cast off 5 stitches right side for armhole and cast off 2 more on row 55. (If carriage is the wrong side for cast off then cast off on rows 54 and 56 instead.) Continue as for back until row 83 to start neck shaping. On row 83 hold 6 stitches on the neck side (opposite side to armhole shaping). Hold 3 stitches on rows 85, 87, 89, 91, 93 and 95. Hold 2 on row 97. (Hold on rows 86, 88, 90, 92, 94, 96 and 98 if carriage is on other side.) Knit 2 rows on remaining unheld 23 stitches for shoulder. Cast off shoulder on row 99.

Change to tension 6, remove second coloured yarn and change to plain knitting. On the 26 neck stitches knit 4 rows. Knit 1 row at tension 7 and 4 more rows at tension 6. Pick up first row of neck hem and cast off.

Repeat for second front, reversing shapings.

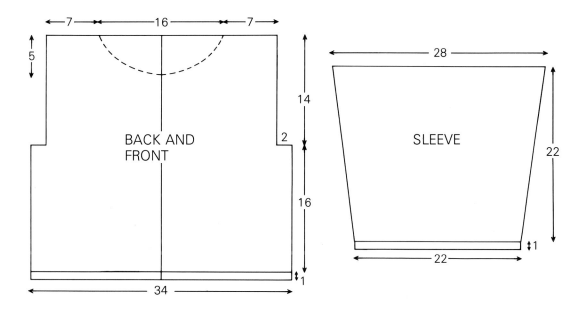

Sleeves: Pick up 92 stitches from the front and back armholes onto needlebed (46 stitches each armhole either side of shoulder seam). Knit in pattern as before, decreasing 1 stitch both sides on row 6 and thereafter every sixth row including row 60 so that on row 61 there are 72 stitches (22cm). Continue knitting until row 72 (22cm). Remove second coloured yarn and change to plain knitting. Change tension to 6 and knit 4 rows. Knit 1 row at tension 7 and 4 more rows at tension 6. Pick up first row of hem and cast off.

Repeat for second sleeve.

Front edging: Pick up 72 stitches down centre front plus 2 each for the top and bottom hems (total 76). Knit 4 rows at tension 6 in black and white yarn. Knit 1 row at tension 7 and 4 more rows at tension 6. Pick up first row of edging and cast off.

Repeat for other front edging.

To finish: Pin and steam press. Pin and then sew seams together edge to edge. Attach 6 press studs to the front edgings. Thread tape or elastic through bottom hem to give a slight gather.

7 Bits and Bobs

Inevitably, after having knitted one or, hopefully, several garments, you will be left with oddments of yarn. What to do with these could be a problem. Darning socks may be a solution – infinitely practical, but boring. Hats, mittens, socks and moccasins which are perfect accessories for any of the preceding outfits solve the problem much better. Knitted mobiles, easy to make and requiring only a small, random selection of yarns also offer an ideal solution.

The hats, which can be knitted in any yarn (although shown here in white cotton and cream wool), are made in four different basic shapes. Infinite variations are possible using any one of these shapes simply by adding earflaps, tassels, pompoms, frills, picot edging or long points which elongate the pattern into 'Wee Willy Winkie' night caps. Just a small selection of the various possibilities are shown here.

The simplest bonnet of all is made from a rectangle of knitting folded in half and sewn down the back with a rouleau threaded through the hem. The next is a shaped bonnet with a picot edge which has rouleaux attached to both corners for tying under the chin. The third, a very basic hat, is a knitted rectangle, gathered at the top and sewn down the shortest seam. And finally, there is a shaped, pointed hat. Both hats are perfectly suited for adding earflaps (with or without a chin strap).

The mittens, socks and moccasins (again shown in white cotton and cream wool) use only two basic patterns. The moccasin has a separate sole and the sock has a seam down the back and along the sole.

Mittens have a habit of getting lost so a substantial collection will prove invaluable. Moreover, they are easy and quick to knit. The mitten pattern is the sock without the heel, and with holes for wrist ribbons or rouleaux.

The socks, moccasins, mittens and mobiles can be made elaborate or simple and rely for their variety on the different yarn, stitch and colour combinations used.

After knitting a successive collection of hats, mittens, socks and mobiles you should have not even the smallest scrap of odd yarn left!

RECTANGULAR BONNET WITH THREADED ROULEAU

Materials
Knitted in Brockwell Wools 4 ply unmercerised white cotton: 25gms. See photo, page 108.

Size
To fit baby aged 0–3 months (50cm). See block diagram for larger sizes.

Tension
Dial number 5
3 stitches = 1cm
4.5 rows = 1cm

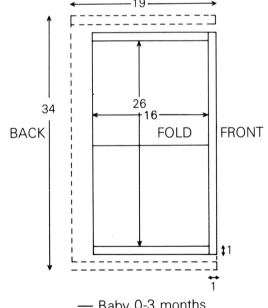

— Baby 0-3 months
--- Baby 6-9 months

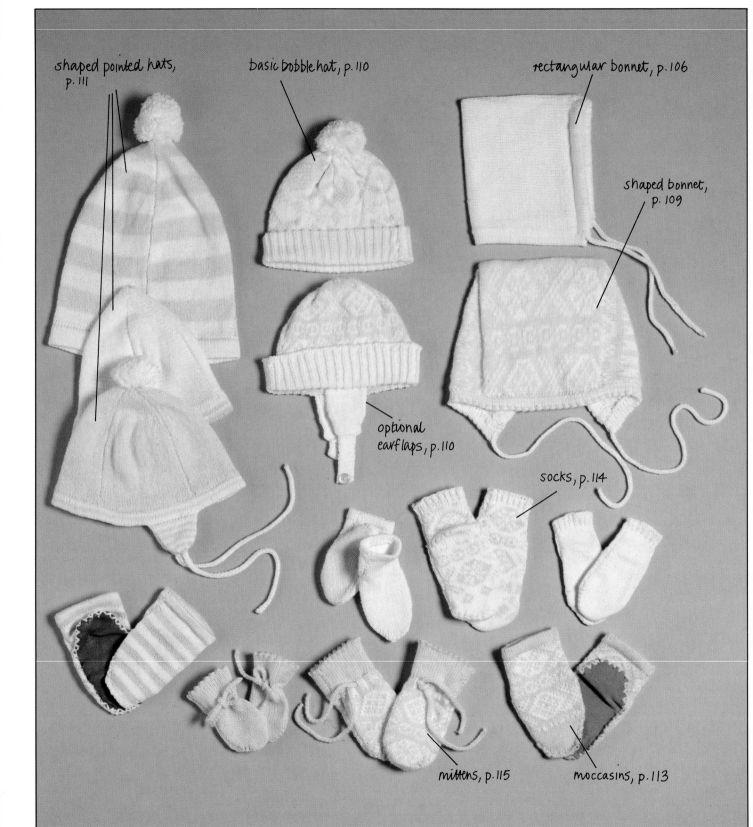

shaped pointed hats, p. 111

basic bobble hat, p. 110

rectangular bonnet, p. 106

shaped bonnet, p. 109

optional earflaps, p. 110

socks, p. 114

mittens, p. 115

moccasins, p. 113

Machines
Any domestic single-bed machine.

Head: Cast on 48 stitches. Knit 5 rows at tension 5, 1 row at tension 6 and 5 rows at tension 5. Pick up cast on row. Knit 117 (26cm) more rows. For the hem, knit the first row with an added, fine contrasting yarn to make identification of the pick-up row easier. Knit 5 rows at tension 5, 1 row at tension 6 and 5 rows at tension 5. Pick up row with contrasting thread. Cast off and remove contrast yarn.

Place the length of knitting onto 84 needles (28cm). Knit hem as before. Pick up first row of hem and cast off.

Rouleau: Cast on 4 stitches. Knit 64cm at tension 5. Cast off.

To finish: Pin and steam press rectangle. Fold in half. Pin the edge with no hem (back of head) and sew seam edge to edge. Thread the rouleau through the front hem.

SHAPED BONNET WITH PICOT EDGE

Materials
Knitted in Brockwell Wools 4 ply unmercerised white cotton: 25gms, and Lister Motoravia 4 ply wool in fisherman: 25gms. See photo, page 108.

Size
To fit baby aged 6–9 months (70cm). See block diagram for other sizes.

Tension
Dial number 6
3.5 stitches = 1cm
5 rows = 1cm
Pattern punchcard in Fair Isle pattern. Use punchcard for baby bag, diagram 23, page 35. Punch card before starting to knit.

Machines
Any domestic single-bed machine with punchcard facility.

Picot edge: Cast on 18 stitches in white cotton and knit 6 rows at tension 5. Knit 1 row at tension 6 and transfer

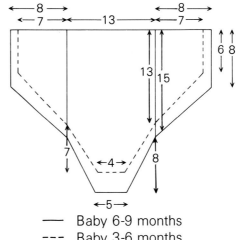

— Baby 6-9 months
--- Baby 3-6 months

alternate stitches to make picot edge. Leave empty needles in knitting position. At tension 5 knit 1 row wool, 2 rows cotton, 1 row wool, 2 rows cotton and pick up first cast on row. Return row counter to 0.

Head: Insert punchcard and knit 2 rows. Begin punchcard on row number 2. Thread second feeder with wool and knit in Fair Isle. On rows 3, 4 and 6 increase 1 stitch both sides. Thereafter increase 1 stitch both sides every third row, until by row 40 (8cm) there are 46 stitches (13cm). Continue knitting Fair Isle for 75 more rows (15cm). Knit several rows of waste yarn. Remove knitting from machine.

Sides: Hook one of the straight sides measuring 15cm onto 52 needles. With carriage set to knit Fair Isle, and wool yarn in second feeder, knit 40 rows (8cm) decreasing 1 stitch both sides on rows 2 and 4. Thereafter decrease 1 stitch both sides every fourth row until there are only 28 stitches left by row 40. Turn carriage to plain knitting, remove second yarn and knit 2 rows cotton, 1 row wool, 2 rows cotton and 1 row wool. Knit 1 row cotton at tension 6. Transfer every alternate stitch to form picot edge, leave empty needles in knitting position, return tension to 5 and knit 6 rows cotton. Pick up first cotton row of hem. Cast off.

Repeat for second side of head.

Rouleaux: Cast on 4 stitches in cotton and at tension 5 knit 20cm. Cast off. Repeat.

To finish: Pin and steam press. Sew shaped back seams first. Attach rouleaux to the two corners.

BASIC BOBBLE HAT
WITH OPTIONAL EARFLAPS

Materials
Knitted in Brockwell Wools 4 ply unmercerised white cotton: 30gms, and Lister Motoravia 4 ply wool in fisherman: 20gms. I pearl button. See photo, page 108.

Size
To fit baby aged 0–3 months (50cm). See block diagram for larger sizes.

Tension
Dial number 5
3 stitches = 1cm
4.2 rows = 1cm

Pattern punchcard in Fair Isle pattern. Use punchcard for baby bag, diagram 23, page 35. Punch card before starting to knit.

Machines
Any domestic single-bed machine with punchcard facility.

Head: Cast on 114 stitches (38cm) in white cotton. Knit 25 rows (6cm). Drop every third stitch and form rib with latchet tool. Insert punchcard. Thread wool through second feeder. Start punchcard on row 2. Knit 52 rows in Fair Isle. Cast off in white cotton.

To finish: Pin flat and steam press. Sew side seams and gather top. Make a white pompom and attach to top.

Earflaps and chin straps: Before finishing, hook 18 stitches from the last row of rib onto the needlebed. Start hooking 18 stitches in from the edge. This will

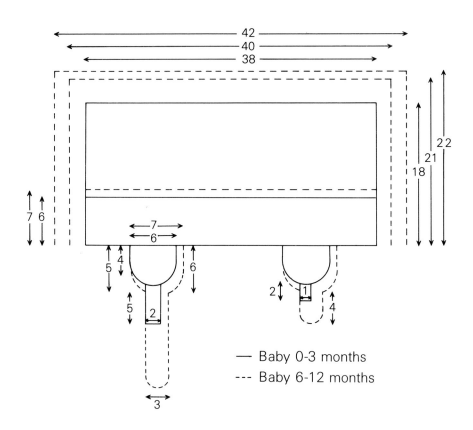

— Baby 0-3 months

--- Baby 6-12 months

leave 42 stitches in the centre in between the two earflaps. In cotton, knit 16 rows at tension 6. On row 17 cast off 2 stitches carriage side and decrease 1 stitch non-carriage side. Repeat on rows 18, 19 and 20 to leave 6 stitches.

For the chin strap, knit 4 rows on these 6 stitches. Transfer the third stitch to make a buttonhole. Knit 4 more rows. Knit 1 row at tension 7, 4 rows at tension 6 and transfer the third stitch for buttonhole. Knit 4 more rows. Pick up first row of strap and cast off.

Repeat for second earflap, hooking onto needlebed 18 stitches from the last row of rib on the hat, starting 18 stitches in from the other edge of the hat.

For the button chin strap, on the remaining 6 stitches at row 20, knit 20 more rows at tension 6. Knit 1 row at tension 7 and 20 rows at tension 6. Pick up first row of strap. Cast off.

To finish: Steam press. Sew up the strap sides. Sew button onto chin strap.

SHAPED POINTED HAT
WITH OPTIONAL EARFLAPS

Materials
Knitted in Brockwell Wools 4 ply unmercerised white cotton: 45gms, and Lister Motoravia 4 ply wool in fisherman: 5gms. See photo, page 108.

Size
To fit baby aged 0–3 months (50cm). See block diagrams for larger sizes.

Tension
Dial number 5
3 stitches = 1cm
4.5 rows = 1cm

Machines
Any domestic single-bed machine.

Head sections: Cast on 27 stitches (9cm). At tension 5 knit 36 rows (8cm) in cotton. Decrease one stitch both sides every third row until by row 72 only 3 stitches remain. Cast off.

Repeat this section another three times.

Match the accessories to the outfit

Hat edging: Hook the cast on row of each of the four sections onto 108 needles (27 stitches each section) with the pearl sides facing. At tension 4, knit 4 rows in cotton, 2 rows in wool, 2 rows in cotton and 2 rows in wool. Knit 1 row in wool at tension 5. At tension 4, knit 2 rows in wool, 2 rows in cotton, 2 rows in wool and 4 rows in cotton. Pick up first row and cast off.

To finish: Pin flat and steam press. Sew sections edge to edge. Add a pompom or a tassel to the pointed top, as required.

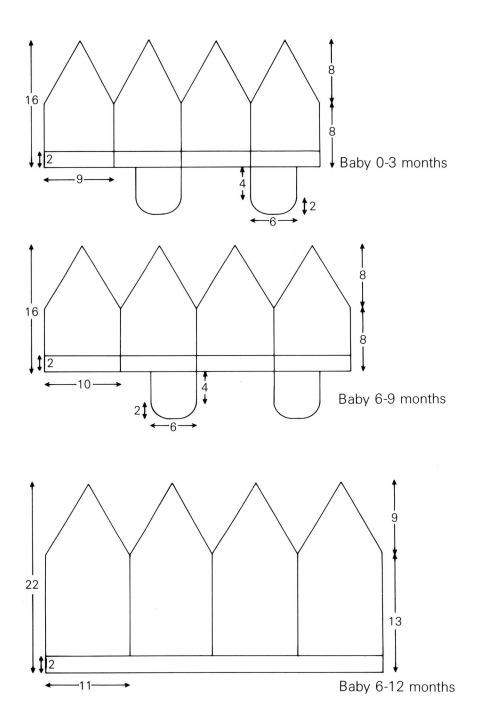

16 · 8 · 8 · 2 · 9 · 4 · 2 · 6 · Baby 0-3 months

16 · 8 · 8 · 2 · 10 · 4 · 2 · 6 · Baby 6-9 months

22 · 9 · 13 · 2 · 11 · Baby 6-12 months

112

Earflaps: From the inside of the hem fold, hook 18 stitches onto the needlebed starting at the edge of a section (see block diagram). At tension 5, knit 16 rows in stripes of 2 rows cotton, 2 rows wool. Decrease 2 stitches carriage side on rows 17, 18, 19, 20, 21, 22 and 23. On the remaining 4 stitches knit 20cm in cotton to form a rouleau tie. Cast off.

Repeat for second earflap. (See block diagram for position of second earflap.)

To finish: Steam press earflaps but not the rouleaux. Sew in the ends of the rouleaux.

MOCCASINS WITH LEATHER SOLES

Materials
Knitted in Brockwell Wools 4 ply unmercerised white cotton: 20gms, and Lister Motoravia 4 ply wool in fisherman: 30gms. Scraps of thin, undyed leather. (Undyed leather will not lose colour when washed.) See photo, page 108.

Size
To fit baby aged 9–18 months (70–90cm). See block diagram for smaller size.

Tension
Dial number 5
3 stitches = 1cm
4.5 rows = 1cm
Pattern punchcard in Fair Isle pattern. Use punchcard for baby bag, diagram 23, page 35. Punch card before starting to knit.

Machines
Any domestic single-bed machine with punchcard facility.

Front: Using wool in main feeder, cast on 12 stitches (4cm). Increase one stitch both sides every 2 rows until row 18 (30 stitches). Thread cotton through second feeder, start punchcard on row 2, and knit 18 rows in Fair Isle. On row 36, decrease one stitch both sides. Repeat on rows 42 and 48. Continue in Fair Isle until row 54. Remove cotton yarn and knit hem in wool. Knit 6 rows at tension 5, 1 row at tension 6 and 6 rows at tension 5. Pick up first row of hem and cast off.

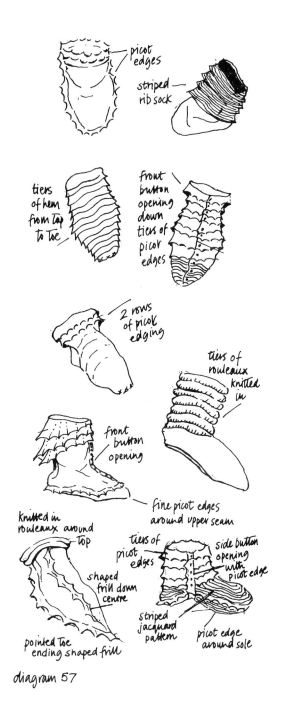

diagram 57

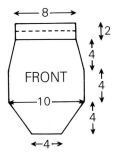

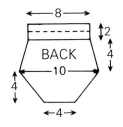

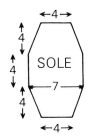

Baby 9-18 months

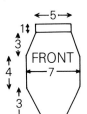

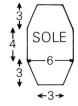

Baby 3-9 months

Back: Cast on 12 stitches in wool. Increase to 30 stitches over 18 rows (4cm) as for front. On row 18, thread cotton through second feeder, start punchcard on row 2, and knit in Fair Isle decreasing one stitch both sides on rows 18, 24 and 30. On row 36, change to knitting in wool only. For the hem, knit 6 rows at tension 5, 1 row at tension 6 and 6 rows at tension 5. Pick up first row of hem and cast off on row 49.

To finish: Steam press and sew the front to the back at the side seams to the point where they meet the soles (5cm). Cut leather for soles to size (see block diagram). Punch holes, if necessary, close to the edge of the soles. Sew knitting to leather soles.

If knitted soles are preferred, knit in wool following the block diagram for measurements. Sew the knitted sole to the rest of the moccasin in cross stitch using cotton or wool doubled.

SOCKS

Materials
Knitted in Brockwell Wools 4 ply unmercerised white cotton: 30gms, and Lister Motoravia 4 ply wool in fisherman: 20gms. See photo, page 108.

Size
To fit baby aged 3–9 months (60–70cm). See block diagram for larger size.

Tension
Dial number 5
3 stitches = 1cm
4.5 rows = 1cm
If a lighter sock is required, use a tighter tension (e.g. 3 or 4) and a finer yarn. Remember to knit another

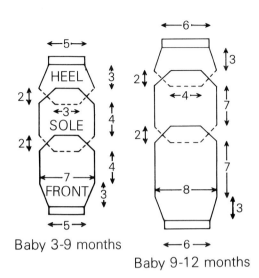

Baby 3-9 months

Baby 9-12 months

To finish: Pin and steam press to uncurl edges. Sew seams edge to edge with white cotton.

NB Both the moccasins and socks can be made much more elaborate with the addition of picot edges (instead of ribs), ripples or fins down the side seams, or padded tops. They can be made knee length by adding extra rows to the tops. See diagram 57, page 113 for further suggestions.

MITTENS

Materials
Knitted in Lister Motoravia 4 ply wool: 35gms fisherman, and Brockwell Wools 4 ply unmercerised white cotton: 15gms. See photo, page 108.

Size
To fit baby aged 9–18 months (70–90cm).

Tension
Dial number 5
3 stitches = 1cm
4.5 rows = 1cm

tension swatch before beginning (the yarn can always be re-used).

Pattern punchcard in Fair Isle pattern. Use punchcard for baby bag, diagram 23, page 35. Punch card before starting to knit.

Machines
Any domestic single-bed machine with punchcard facility.

Sock: Cast on 15 stitches (5cm) in cotton. At tension 5 knit 6 rows. Drop alternate stitches and form rib with latchet tool. Thread wool through second feeder, start punchcard on row 2, and knit 4 rows in Fair Isle. On rows 10, 15 and 21 increase one stitch both sides. On row 22 remove wool and knit in cotton. For heel, hold 1 needle both sides on rows 22, 24, 26, 27, 28 and 29. Knit 1 row. On rows 31 to 36, push back into knitting position the held needles (two by two beginning with the inside needles). Knit to row 58 (still in cotton only).

Shape toe by holding pairs of outside needles on rows 58, 60, 62, 64, 66 and 68. Push back into knitting position pairs of held needles (beginning with the inside pair) on rows 70, 72, 74, 76, 78 and 80. Thread wool through second feeder, start punchcard on row 2, and knit in Fair Isle to row 98. On rows 98, 104 and 110, decrease 1 stitch both sides. Knit to row 113. Change to cotton only and knit 6 rows for the rib. Drop alternate stitches and form rib with latchet tool. Cast off.

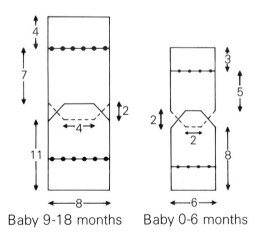

Baby 9-18 months   Baby 0-6 months

If a lighter mitten is required, use a tighter tension (e.g. 3 or 4) and use a finer yarn. Remember to knit another tension swatch before beginning (the yarn can always be re-used).

Pattern punchcard in Fair Isle pattern. Use punchcard for baby bag, diagram 23, page 35. Punch card before starting to knit.

Machines
Any domestic single-bed machine with a punchcard facility.

Front and back: Cast on 24 stitches (8cm) in wool. Knit 18 rows (4cm) at tension 5. Knit one row at tension 6. Transfer every alternate needle for picot edge. Leave empty needles in knitting position and change tension to 5. Knit 18 more rows. On row 37, pick up cast on row, knit one row and transfer every fourth stitch, beginning on the second from the left (thereby making 6 holes for the tie).

On row 39 thread cotton through second feeder. Insert punchcard and start punchcard on row 2. Knit in Fair Isle. On rows 69, 70 and 71, hold 1 stitch both sides. On rows 72, 73, 74, 75, 76 and 77 hold 1 stitch alternate sides. Knit 1 row. On rows 79 to 84, push back 1 needle alternate sides nearest centre. On rows 85, 86 and 87 push back 1 stitch both sides nearest centre.

Continue knitting in Fair Isle until row 119. Transfer every fourth stitch, beginning second row from left (to make 6 holes). Remove cotton from second feeder and knit 18 rows in wool only. Knit 1 row at tension 6. Transfer every alternate stitch for picot edge. Leave empty needles in knitting position. Knit 18 more rows. Pick up first row of hem (first non-Fair Isle row). Cast off.

If Fair Isle is required only on one face of mitten, change to wool only at row 78.

If *matching* Fair Isle is required for both faces of mitten then at row 79 make a note of the punchcard row number when Fair Isle began and ended, (e.g. started punchcard on row 2, finished on row 32). Mark punchcard on reverse side at row 32. Remove punchcard and insert back to front and upside down. Wind forward 5 rows from marked row 32 and knit as for front.

Rouleaux: Cast on 3 stitches in wool. With tension at 5 knit for 36cm. Cast off. Repeat.

To finish: Steam press. Sew in ends. Sew seams edge to edge. Sew outsides and insides of the hems separately. Thread rouleaux through holes.

Elastic (cut and sewn to baby's wrist size) or ribbon can be used very effectively instead of the knitted rouleaux.

MOBILES

Materials
Knitted in any variety of yarns: 25gms.

Tension
Dial number 5
3 stitches = 1cm
4.5 rows = 1cm

Machines
Any domestic single-bed machine.

Even spiral: Cast on 10 stitches. Knit 4 rows. Hold 1 needle on non-carriage side, knit 4 rows. Repeat holding 1 needle and knitting 4 rows until 40 rows have been knitted and all the needles are on hold. Push all needles back into knitting position. This constitutes one section.

Repeat the full section a minimum of 5 more times (240 rows) for a satisfactory spiral effect. Cast off the 10 stitches. Change yarns after each section.

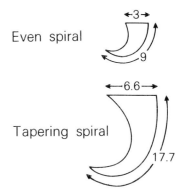

Even spiral

Tapering spiral

To finish: Sew in ends. Press and starch (if necessary). Fix a thread of nylon or wool to one end and let it hang within a baby's sight or reach.

Tapering spiral (50gms): Cast on 20 stitches. Knit 4 rows. Hold one needle non-carriage side, knit 4 rows. Repeat holding 1 needle and knitting 4 rows until 80 rows have been knitted and all the needles are on hold. Push all needles into knitting position. Cast off one stitch carriage side. This constitutes one section.

Repeat section, with the number of rows decreasing by 4 rows each time until the final section should be knitted over 24 rows on 5 needles. Cast off the 5 stitches.

To finish: Sew in ends. Press and starch (if necessary). Fix a thread of nylon or wool to the cast on end so that the spiral decreases towards the bottom.

NB The spirals can be varied enormously by using coloured or textured yarns and combinations of stiff and stretchy yarns. The size of the spiral can also be changed completely by casting on more stitches and knitting more sections. See experimental swatches in Chapter 8, page 118, for further suggestions.

8 Experiments

By now, after following instructions for basic blocks using plain, striped, intarsia, lace and Fair Isle knitting, the experienced knitter and the ambitious beginner alike must surely welcome the opportunity to experiment. This chapter is for them, or indeed any knitter who wishes to try their tweedy baby in wonderful, warm, blister and cable stitch constructions, their outrageous baby in extravagant ripples, their sporty baby in shock-absorbent padded materials and their sophisti-cated or traditional baby in intricate and elaborate tuck and lace knitting.

All these ideas and many other experiments could be explored. Four ideas are illustrated by garment examples with swatch instructions and the rest are variations on these four.

The ultimate aim is to inspire the knitter to create totally original garments perfectly suited to the special baby they are knitting for.

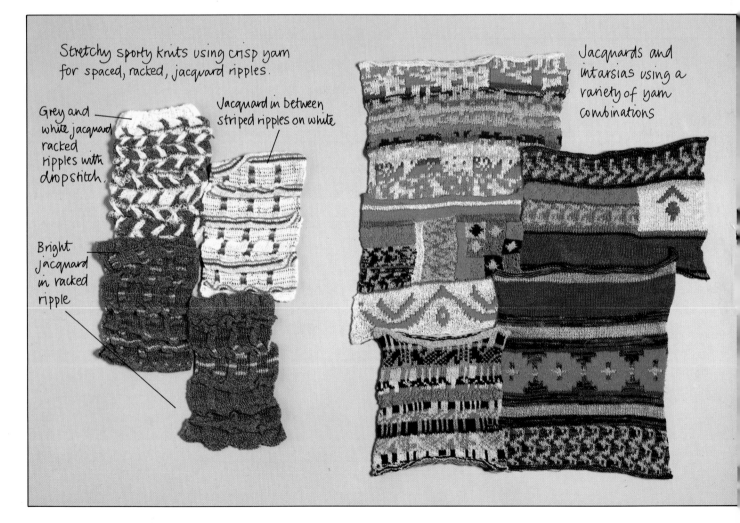

Stretchy sporty knits using crisp yarn for spaced, racked, jacquard ripples.

Grey and white jacquard racked ripples with drop stitch.

Jacquard in between striped ripples on white

Bright jacquard in racked ripple

Jacquards and intarsias using a variety of yarn combinations

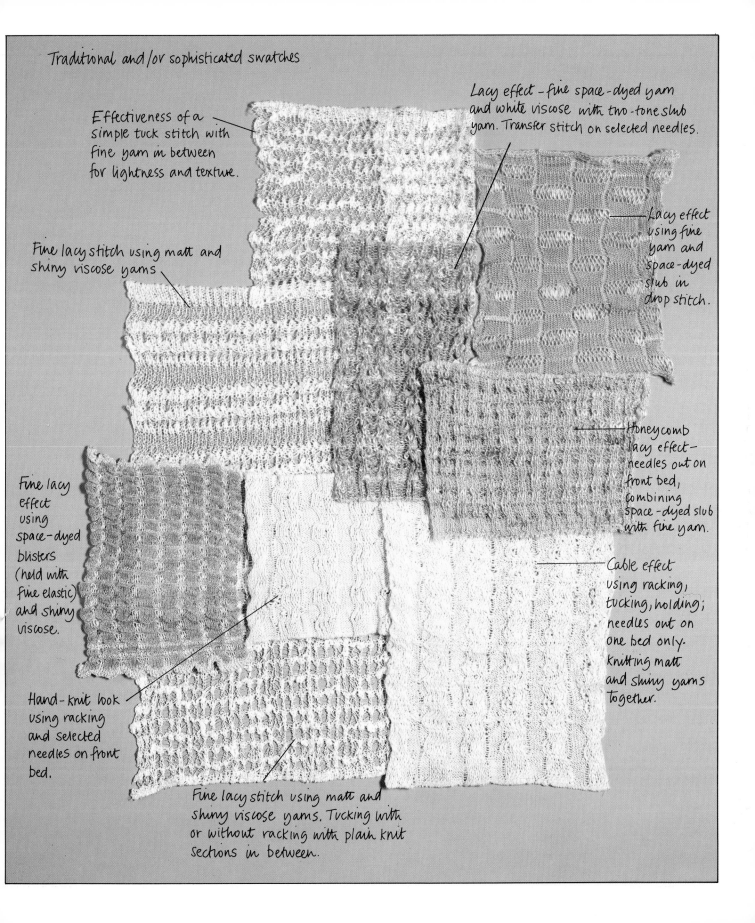

Traditional and/or sophisticated swatches

Effectiveness of a simple tuck stitch with fine yarn in between for lightness and texture.

Lacy effect - fine space-dyed yarn and white viscose with two-tone slub yarn. Transfer stitch on selected needles.

Fine lacy stitch using matt and shiny viscose yarns

Lacy effect using fine yarn and space-dyed slub in drop stitch.

Fine lacy effect using space-dyed blisters (held with fine elastic) and shiny viscose.

Honeycomb lacy effect — needles out on front bed, combining space-dyed slub with fine yarn.

Cable effect using racking, tucking, holding; needles out on one bed only. Knitting matt and shiny yarns together.

Hand-knit look using racking and selected needles on front bed.

Fine lacy stitch using matt and shiny viscose yarns. Tucking with or without racking with plain knit sections in between.

Tweedy swatches. Animal skin effects, subtle tweed effects, surface effects, embroidery, threaded leather, use of reverse sides, padding, etc.

Reverse of swatch on right

Using racking, this tweedy, ripple-striped, fine bouclé in navy and two tweed yarns gives an animal skin effect.

Embroidered jacquard in white and tweed. Fine drop stitch. Net sewn to reverse side.

Racked version of held stitch pattern using furry yarns, tweed and black for animal skin effect.

Tweedy padded soft tubular swatch, using tubular knitting in soft tweed yarn padded with soft wool roving.

Same stitch as swatch at top right. Different effect through use of solid colours.

Fading-out effect achieved by subtle striping of yarns from light to dark.

Furry and tweed yarns combined in held stitch pattern using leather ribbon.

All suitable for jerseys, jackets, coats, etc.

Striped tweedy chenille jacquard.

Surface tweedy effect - woven in swatch pattern achieved by subtle striping of yarns from light to dark.

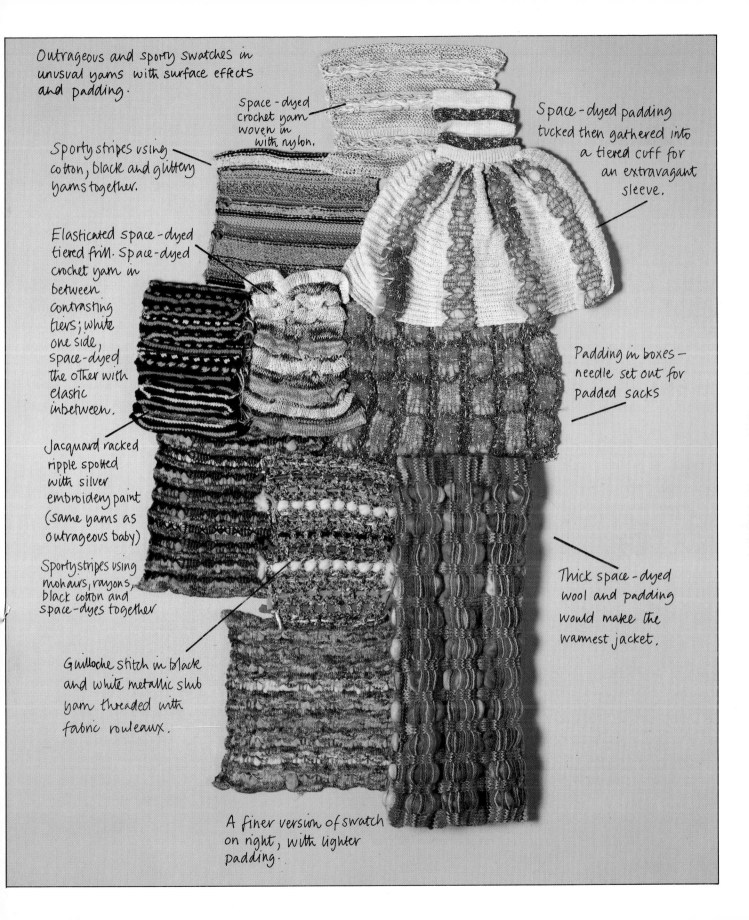

Outrageous and sporty swatches in unusual yarns with surface effects and padding.

Space-dyed crochet yarn woven in with nylon.

Space-dyed padding tucked then gathered into a tiered cuff for an extravagant sleeve.

Sporty stripes using cotton, black and glittery yarns together.

Elasticated space-dyed tiered frill. Space-dyed crochet yarn in between contrasting tiers; white one side, space-dyed the other with elastic inbetween.

Jacquard racked ripple spotted with silver embroidery paint (same yarns as outrageous baby)

Padding in boxes — needle set out for padded sacks

Sporty stripes using mohairs, rayons, black cotton and space-dyes together

Thick space-dyed wool and padding would make the warmest jacket.

Guilloche stitch in black and white metallic slub yarn threaded with fabric rouleaux.

A finer version of swatch on right, with lighter padding.

CHRISTENING DRESS/SHAWL

Swatch combining double-bed openwork lace-effect stitch and single-bed tuck stitch.

The tuck stitch here, though very simple, is most effective as a part of an original stitch combination. Both these stitches and variations on them are ideal for knitting in thicker mercerised cotton for an expensive sophisticated summer dress or in white as part of a traditional matinée jacket.

Materials

Brockwell Wools singles (2/30s mercerised cotton) cream, and white (2/30s) viscose. Knitted together through the same feeder they knit as 2 ply.

Tension

Dial number 2 (double-bed swatch)
3.5 stitches = 1 cm
5.5 rows = 1 cm

Machines

Any double-bed machine and a single-bed machine.

Swatch: Cast on 40 stitches back bed only and knit one row at tension 4. Transfer sets of 5 stitches to the front bed, leaving sets of 4 stitches on the back bed in between (see diagram 58). Change to tension 2 and knit one row. After every 2 rows rack one space to the right until the machine will rack no further. Then after every 2 more rows rack all the way to the left. Repeat racking all the way to the right, then all the way to the

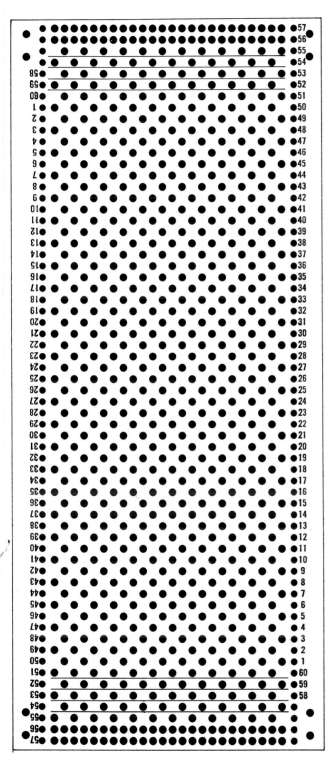

left. After 55 rows (10cm) change to tension 3. Knit one row, transfer all stitches to the back bed. Knit several rows in waste yarn and remove knitting from machine.

Steam press carefully and lay flat. To gather, place 2 stitches from the last row before the waste yarn onto 20 needles (see diagram 59). Knit at tension 3 on back bed only, in cotton and viscose together. If more gathering is required, place 3 or more stitches on every needle.

This lacy knitting will need to be gathered onto some plain knitting for a finished garment or onto a piece of knitting with a simple tuck stitch pattern in the same yarn (honeycomb pattern). Having gathered above swatch onto needlebed, knit 1 row at tension 3. Then, tuck stitch using punchcard and single-bed machine (see diagram 60).

diagram 58

back bed — single bed cast on tension 4

front bed — transfer sets of 5 stitches onto front bed leaving sets of 4 stitches on back bed

back bed

diagram 59

2 stitches on every needle

remove waste yarn after pairs of stitches cast onto needles

diagram 60

123

PADDED JACKET

Swatch using circular knitting (double-bed machine) with padding inserted after each circular section has been knitted.

This swatch can appear very rich and sophisticated by using white only or by changing to very dark colours. For example, try it knitted in white or black mohair. (However, avoid using very hairy yarns if the garment is for a young baby as he or she may choke or develop a skin allergy to the fluff.) For practical purposes, the padded knitting is perfect used as knee pads, or even as a padded helmet to protect the most adventurous baby.

Materials
Brightly coloured slub linen 4 ply in magenta, blue, orange, turquoise. Padding: 2cm-deep nylon roving (wool or Terylene roving would also be suitable; if it is too thick it can easily be separated into the right size strips).

Tension
Dial number 6
2.75 stitches = 1cm
4.5 rows = 1cm (Multiply this by 2 when using a row counter as the swatch is done on circular knitting.)
Each section = 12 rows circular, one row both beds.

Machines
Any double-bed machine.

Swatch: Cast on both beds with 20 needles on each. Knit 3 rows circular, one row both beds. *Knit 12 rows circular, open beds and insert roving. Make sure that it is pushed well down in order to avoid catching on the needles. Close beds, knit one row both beds.** Repeat from * to **.

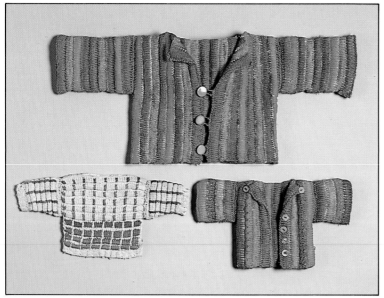

RIPPLED JACKET

Swatch combining ripples, jacquard, racking and striping on a double-bed machine.

The interest of this swatch lies mainly in the surface effect produced by the stitch construction and the use of bright colours. In dark or neutral colours it could be equally interesting and completely different; more suited to a tweedy baby perhaps.

Materials
2 ply black cotton and 2 ply white cotton combined in the same feeder. 4 ply green, yellow, orange, turquoise, pink and emerald green cotton.

Tension
Dial number 5.5 (both beds)
3 stitches = 1cm
9.4 rows = 1cm
26 rows (i.e. stitch pattern sequence) = 2.7cm
Rib: 3 × 2 rib tension 4 both beds. (See diagram 61 for needle layout.)

diagram 61

back bed
needles out of action for rib

rib 3×2 rib

needle set out, use tension 4 both beds

front bed needles out of action for rib

diagram 62

needle set out back bed
needle set out front bed

pushers set out

Machines

A double-bed machine (Passap).

Swatch: See diagram 62, page 125 for needle set out. After knitting rib (see diagram 61) change to tension 5.5. Place stitches from the row before last onto the empty needles on the front bed. Pattern sequence is as follows:

*2 rows N/N (knit) black and white yarns combined. Rack one turn to right. 4 rows GX/N (back bed not knitting) black and white. Rack one turn to right. 2 rows GX/N in coloured yarn. Rack one turn to right. 4 rows GX/N black and white yarn. Rack one turn to right. 2 rows N/N black and white yarn. Rack one turn to right. 2 rows GX/N black and white yarn. Rack one turn to left. 2 rows GX/BX in coloured yarn (patterning using pushers on front bed only). Rack one turn to left. 2 rows GX/BX in black and white. Rack one turn to left. 2 rows GX/BX in coloured yarn. Rack one turn to left. 4 rows GX/N in black and white yarn. Rack one turn to left.**

Repeat from * to **.

FANCY JERSEY

Swatch combining blisters and cables.

Materials

3 ply bouclé, 4 ply flecked mohair, 3 ply silk-effect yarn. (When combined, the ply is a little heavier than a double knitting yarn.) 4 ply soft, shiny cotton, a twisted shiny and matt wool/viscose yarn, and a chenille. Much of the interest of the swatch lies in the yarn combination as well as the stitch.

Tension

Dial number 6. In a complicated stitch construction it is easier to measure the tension swatch from the beginning of the stitch sequence to the end.

In this example, a 17 row repeat = 5cm
Cable of 6 stitches = 4cm
Plain knitting over 6 stitches = 4cm, therefore 1.5 stitches = 1cm, 3.4 rows = 1cm.

This is only one example; inevitably the tension measurements will vary according to the yarns and machines used. Try using different yarn combinations and placing of cable to vary the design.

Machines

Any chunky single-bed machine.

Swatch: Cast on 20 stitches. Knit 4 rows at tension 6 using a combination of first 3 yarns (purple). Knit 1 row 4 ply shiny cotton (red) at tension 10 (to facilitate cable). Cable over the 6 central stitches (leaving 7 stitches both sides). Change to tension 6 and knit 4 more rows in yarn combination (purple). Knit 1 row 4 ply cotton (red). Knit 2 rows of the twisted yarn (blue) and 2 rows in chenille (black). Knit 2 rows twisted yarn (blue). Pick up 7 stitches of first row of twisted yarn (blue) both sides of swatch, leaving the cabled section. Knit 1 row in 4 ply (red).

Repeat.

Suppliers' List

The yarns used, or their equally good equivalents, are available in retail knitting/craft shops or department stores.

The following companies supplied all the yarns used in the book and also provide a mail order service.

Argyll Wools Limited, PO Box 15, Priestley Mills, Pudsey, W. Yorks LS28 9LT.

British Mohair Spinners Limited, PO Box 58, Midland Mills, Valley Road, Bradford, W. Yorks BD1 4RL.

Brockwell Wools, Stansfield Mill, Stansfield Mill Lane, Triangle, Sowerby Bridge, W. Yorks HX6 3LZ.

Lister and Company, Manningham Mills, Bradford, W. Yorks BD9 4SH.

Patons and Baldwins (Matlock) Limited, Derwent Mills, Matlock, Derbyshire DE4 3FR.

Rowan Yarns, Green Lane Mill, Washpit, Holmfirth, W. Yorks HD7 1RW.

Silverknit, Park Road, Calverton, Nottingham, Notts NG14 6LL.

Acknowledgements

Thanks to Josie Walters for her hours of patient knitting; to the mothers Esther Pearson, Sara Ansah, Carol Sparks, Lynne Green and Hermione Skrine, and their beautiful children Morgan, Niall, Laura, Catherine and Una; and to baby Alex. Thanks also to Muriel Gascoin and Gill Clack for editorial work, Peter Hutchings for photography and Jill Leman for book design.